D0779406

Godless
GRACE

Godless GRACE

*How Nonbelievers Are
Making the World
Safer, Richer and Kinder*

by **David I. Orenstein**, Ph.D.
Linda Ford Blaikie, L.C.S.W.

HUMANIST PRESS
WASHINGTON, DC

Dedication

....

The authors wish to dedicate this book to the memory of
Bertrand Russell; a man whose ideas so many have relied on, both
past and present, to inform their humanism, support their honest
inquiry and feed their freethought and skepticism.

Table of Contents

················

Acknowledgements

....

IT GOES WITHOUT saying that this book, as it was originally imagined and in how it evolved, would not have been possible without the hard work and collaborative efforts of my co-author, Linda Ford Blaikie. Others need to be recognized as well. Good friend and French atheist Michel Bougois was an early interviewee before the book's focus became boots-on-the-ground humanitarianism. I'd like to offer a deep "thank you" to my friend, Dr. Phil Zuckerman, for his wonderful foreword. I also cannot thank enough David Silverman, the President of American Atheists, for writing the visionary afterword and Pam Whissel, also of American Atheists, for her editorial review of the early manuscript. Lastly, I offer a hearty thank you to Luis Granados, Jessica Xiao, Matt Cerami, Jan Melchior, and Merrill Miller, as well as the other staff at the Humanist Press, for their ongoing support.

All of the wonderful humanist activists interviewed are each owed a debt of gratitude and need to be lauded for their work to make the world a safer, richer, and kinder place. I also give thanks to all my dear friends in New York City Atheists who hold by common cause both healthy doubt and honest questioning of faith, while at the same time focusing on why legally, politically, and emotionally we nonbelievers must stand together for secularism.

But the most important thanks go to the five women in my life who have shaped my worldview, supported me spiritually, and served as my muses for the two years it took to complete this book. To Francesca, Chloe, Melissa, Emily, and Judy, you are each my world, and the locus of joy and love I feel toward all of you keeps me grounded, human, and humane. You are each, in your own special way, my "Supreme Being."

Dr. David I. Orenstein, August 2015

MY DEEP GRATITUDE goes to David Orenstein for coming up with the fascinating project of interviewing atheists doing humanitarian work across the globe and for trusting me to conduct and compose those interviews.

Thanks also to Kenneth Bronstein for inviting me to run a monthly Recovering from Religion support group for New York City Atheists, which I ran for five years. This is where I met David Orenstein and many other inspirational and brave seekers.

Psychologist Dr. Darrel W. Ray who founded the support groups that now exist throughout the United States deserves a big shout-out for creating a space where people can feel less alone as they struggle with leaving their religions and also for establishing the Secular Therapy Project, an online resource where atheists can locate secular psychotherapists.

There are no bounds to my gratitude and admiration for my son, Dana, who is a humanitarian at his core. He is an example of how a difficult life can shape a person into a giver rather than a taker.

And to the participants in Chapter 1, our conversations have enlarged and enriched me beyond description. What more could one ask for? I hope that I have done you justice.

Linda Ford Blaikie, L.C.S.W., August 2015

Foreword

....

BY DR. PHIL ZUCKERMAN

PROFESSOR OF SOCIOLOGY, PITZER COLLEGE

IT'S NOT THAT we can't cook, it's not that we walk funny, or that we are way too into cats. I've never heard any of these stereotypes or negative assumptions concerning secular people. What I have heard, however, and many times—as I am sure every other atheist/agnostic in America has also heard many times—is that we have no morals.

Without question, the main stereotype or negative association, when it comes to nonbelievers, is this: immorality. Without belief in God (our fellow Americans often wonder and assert) how can we be good people? Impossible!

This all-too-common linkage of secularity with immorality runs quite deep, and it has real-world consequences. For example, in various national surveys in which a random sample of Americans was asked if they would hypothetically vote for a presidential candidate who was black, Jewish, homosexual, female, Hispanic, Muslim, etc.—atheist came in last place. One such survey found that 43 percent of Americans wouldn't vote for an atheist for president.[1] Another survey found that atheists come in last place when Americans are asked to rank members of various racial, ethnic, or religious groups as potential spouses for their kids.[2] Thus, in the words of sociologist

Penny Edgell, "atheists are at the top of the list of groups that Americans find problematic."[3]

Additional studies reveal just how disliked the nonreligious are.[4] One recent study found that people gave lower priority to atheist or agnostic patients than to Christian patients when asked to hypothetically rank them on a waiting list to receive a kidney.[5] Another legal study has documented the degree to which atheist parents have been denied custody rights in the wake of a divorce.[6]

And yes, what ultimately underlies this widespread distaste for the godless, according to the analyses of psychologists Marcel Harper and Will Gervais, is that many Americans consider secular people to be—you guessed it—immoral.[7]

What is going on here? Why do so many people consider atheism and agnosticism to be akin to immorality? From where does this negative association arise? We can only speculate.

One possible cause might have to do with sheer historical inertia; religion—as a dominant societal force—has been people trumpeting its moral superiority for thousands of years, proclaiming and instituting a monopoly on the matter, and castigating all competition (other religions or no religion at all) as morally inferior or amoral. When people are told by the powers that be, generation after generation, that religion is the sole source arbiter of morality, they tend to believe it—no matter how dubious the assertion.

Whatever the cause, we need to deconstruct it. Get rid of it. We do that by 1) coming out as secular, and 2) debunking the stereotype with facts and examples to the contrary. As for the first— and as our gay and lesbian brothers and sisters have so admirably shown—nothing does more to snuff out stigma and dispel unkind stereotypes than simply coming out—letting your family, friends, neighbors, and co-workers know who and what you are. I am confident that as the number of secular Americans continues to grow, and as more and more of these secular Americans—moms, dads, teachers, firemen, soccer coaches, nurses, senators, sergeants, etc.—come out, people will see that we are (on average) decent, upstanding, and ethical individuals. And the linkage of atheism, agnosticism, and secularity with immorality will be harder and harder to sustain in more and more people's minds.

But we also need to aggressively debunk the immorality matter with hard facts, bright examples, and heroic stories that reveal the best of our secular moral selves. By highlighting our moral potential, by showcasing the extreme good that we do for this world—both locally and globally—and by exposing the underlying motivations as well as the awesome accomplishments of deeply secular people who are deeply moral, we help dispel the myth of secular immorality. But this book does more than that. What the stories and profiles presented in the pages that follow ultimately do—and where they are most successful—is to offer inspiration.

May you be as inspired by the pages ahead as I am.

········

Our Journeys to Godlessness

....

DR. DAVID I. ORENSTEIN

MANY BELIEVERS HAVE asked me why I choose activist atheism over agnosticism or just quiet general nonbelief. My simple response is always the same: Just as the religious hold dear their beliefs regarding faith and want to spread the "good news" of their religion, I, too, have the same interest and the same civil rights to share my values and ideas with others. Although this book is not autobiographical, both the interviewees and readers of this work should know the authors' perceptions, history, and perspective. Since full disclosure requires a certain level of honesty, it is important to share my nontheism openly and proudly.

I am an apostate. I became an atheist consciously at the age of eight. I think I chose not to believe because I never really thought the supernatural was special in any way. Don't get me wrong, I had and still have an active imagination, and I loved reading comic books about the exploits of Superman and his ilk. But religion, religious ritual, and god-belief never seemed to make sense to me from a practical point of view.

As I look back on my choice, I think that I've always been a person without religious faith. However, I do have faith in humanity, and I remain optimistic even though there are plenty of reasons for great sadness in our world. I conclude at its core and through its roots, this sadness is caused by some form of religious philosophy, sectarian violence, or god-worship.

But let's get back to my atheist journey. When I was a preteen, I became ill with rheumatic fever. The infection left me with both a damaged mitral and aortic valve. I thought if there was a god, and if he was a kind and loving deity, then why would he hurt me so? After all, as a child, I never did anything to hurt him or anyone. Who plans this way? Why, if God controls all, did I have to suffer or for that matter why does anyone have to suffer? If God is so powerful, why not just fix everything? Then I realized in my own words, what Woody Allen said years before (although I didn't know he had made this statement at the time), "It's not that God isn't all-powerful, it's just that he is an underachiever." As a fellow Jew from Brooklyn, the joke and the pathos of Allen's comment resonates with me.

So in 1979, at the age of seventeen, I underwent open-heart surgery to replace my aortic valve. They put in a porcine valve (a fancy way of saying "pig"). I was no longer Kosher (not that I ever really was), but at least my short life was extended a little longer. That was, up until 1987, when the porcine valve calcified and was replaced by a non-organic valve. After each surgery, I was told that my family and friends prayed for my survival. Each time I went under the knife, I neither prayed nor pleaded with "God" to spare me. Frankly, I was more concerned with the job experience of the heart surgeon.

I guess you can say that my heart surgeries were a form of battle, and in that case I can assure you that there are atheists in foxholes, because I am and will always be a nonbeliever. I choose atheism because I have never seen evidence to contradict my conclusion that there isn't a God. So if God does not exist, it follows that there is no need for a religious or religiously based spiritual life. It also follows that one can and will act morally and with kindness toward others even without the threat or reliance on God or a theistic philosophy. The scientist and skeptic Carl Sagan is quoted as saying, "Extraordinary claims require extraordinary evidence." Without evidence, humans backslide into a Paleolithic set of beliefs which existed way before science could show us that the natural world and the mechanics of the universe are knowable. The physical world can be, and is, beautiful and testable. And the most wonderful part of it all is that it can be understood through human invention and inquiry. Although there is still so much more to know, science allows us to both explore and expand our knowledge of the natural world, and that it is both beautiful and amazing. The daily discoveries in all scientific disciplines show us how the world and universe operate without the need for superstitious belief or theistic intervention. At the same time we have religion, which tells us nothing about human nature, other than that we can be ignorant, sometimes violent, and duped into believing the unbelievable through religious dogma and ritual, which is actually really good only for those who get paid to lead a flock.

What I knew as a little boy I know as an adult man. There is no need for any god. We have science and literature and fine arts and so many human-made intellectual contrivances that heighten our sensibilities. We also have the scientific method to fill in the gaps of our understanding and, more importantly, to explore what we don't know. As long as we can test the mechanics of the universe we can ensure that what we do know is valid while continuing to question and continue to make discoveries to enliven our world.

LINDA FORD BLAIKIE

AS FAR BACK AS I can recall my mother told me that the Virgin Mary was my real mother and that she, my biological mother, was simply fostering me here on Earth. A miraculous medal hung around my neck, and my care was left in God's hands. My mother tended to earthly needs—as she saw them. She was severely emotionally disturbed, but I took the whole thing seriously—praying frequently for guidance and wisdom and kneeling at the altar in humility and reverence. Religion in many ways saved me from succumbing to my mother's influence and gave me the courage that I needed to fly solo, but it wasn't until an LSD trip at the age of 18 that I realized this courage was inside me, and there was in fact no God.

That realization left me bereft for three long years. I was alone, estranged from my crazy family, working my way through college, and in daily, if not hourly, moments of panic. I would reflexively begin to pray and as my hands would move together, I would remember that I no longer believed in God or Mary and would have to white-knuckle it alone. Eventually, as with any loss, I moved on and am thankful for the imaginary protection I shepherded myself with. Who knows what would have happened without it. But at what cost?

I believed, like all Catholics did at the time and as many still do, that to think "bad" thoughts was a sin, almost as wrong as committing the bad act itself. With God's protection from life's terrors comes God's threat for the disobedient. If you don't obey you go to hell. It was a terrifying thought that nuns would serve up in graphic, gory detail. My mother beat me, and I wished her dead. I couldn't help it. I couldn't control those thoughts. Now, having been a psychotherapist for forty years, I can tell you that having those wishes stopped me from retaliating in deed against my mother. Those thoughts of revenge were healthy. They allowed me to process my rage at my mother. What's more, sharing those thoughts was a release valve. People who feel fearful and guilty about their thoughts are in danger of acting out unconsciously, sometimes in deadly ways, and sometimes not even against the perpetrator.

For example, some years ago, I heard a radio interview of a serial killer in New England. From time to time, he had inexplicable and irresistible urges to murder young girls at the college where his mother worked. As it turned out, his mother would flatter and preen over these girls while at the same time belittling and emasculating her son. It wasn't until he went into therapy and realized his murderous wishes were actually against his mother, not the girls she showered praise over, that he stopped killing and turned himself in—several innocent victims later.

I was lucky to have the "blessing" in childhood of an imaginary protector, and I was lucky to be able to jettison that imagined protection as I entered adulthood. Standing alone, without God, allowed me to develop into a centered being who owned her thoughts and feelings. I became whole, instead of a dissociated being who could not trust my own inner roadmap. I struggled with my fear of death without relying on an afterlife, and I have arrived at a place of peace as I face life's challenges. I have been privileged to help others as my life's work, and in giving to others my life developed texture, depth and meaning—a very rich journey indeed.

*The etymologist finds the
deadest words to have been
once a brilliant picture.
Language is fossil poetry.*

– Ralph Waldo Emerson

Introduction

GRACE ISN'T ALWAYS easy to define, but when you have the good fortune to be in the presence of grace, it is unmistakable. One can be left humbled and even awestruck. Life suddenly feels richer, fuller, and more meaningful. One feels less alienated, less alone, and more connected.

Some people experience grace as divine, as coming from elsewhere, from heaven, or from a God. And in its modern usage, thanks mostly to Saint Augustine (354-430 CE) and his heralded publication, *De gratia Christi et de peccato originali (On the Grace of Christ and on Original Sin),* the word grace usually conjures up some kind of religious imagery.

But the word grace need not always have a religious connotation or spiritual connection. According to the Oxford English Dictionary, the word grace—or gracier—reappeared in the French language in the early fourteenth century, where its secular definition was simply to give thanks or remit from punishment.[8] It is the root of words like graceful, gracious, or gracias—gratitude, gratify, and charisma. In its equally historic post-Enlightenment meaning, grace is a word that acknowledges that we should be humble and present for the people we help and for those who help us in return.

The word is important because it defines many of those profiled in this book. There are those who, at this very moment, are doing the gracious good work of alleviating the suffering of others without fanfare or praise. They are attempting to heal the planet in some way by helping our natural environment or the cultural environments that we have created. They are feeding the hungry, healing the sick, or fighting for the human and civil rights of those in communities both local and foreign.

These activists are each doing their good work not for religious or doctrinal reasons—and not to fulfill a dogma or to please an authority. Their work is performed through an intrinsic empathy and reasoned sense of fairness; they hope to eradicate injustice and help others live a better life. They are helping strangers breathe cleaner air, receive social and medical services, support themselves emotionally and financially, gain the right to control their bodies, or love who they wish. They are advocating inside and outside of closed and strict societies so that each citizen may think, write, gather, and discuss their ideas freely both with kindred spirits and with those who would disagree with them.

In Part One, we have chronicled a sampling of some of those atheist humanitarians who spend much of their stay on Earth fighting for the disenfranchised and the unlucky. Some of these secular activists feel atheism is necessary for a better world and others don't. Some are driven by a big heart, some by a warrior spirit, some by the desire to save others from the pain of a shared oppression, and some by the values learned from family. Reading about their experiences and life stories offers us an opportunity to understand the personal motivation of those humanists who choose to help others. But their choices to "be the change" require context.

Part Two provides that context by discussing the history of freethought as well as the current demographic shifts occurring worldwide that impact the secular humanist movement.

This provides clarity regarding the "who, what, where, when, how, and why" of the modern humanist activist movement, which is growing into such an important and far-reaching global force. Part 2 seeks to explain why so many laypeople are choosing to define their nonfaith not just as a strict "I don't believe in god," but as an ethical proposition to improve the lives of others.

WHY IS THIS AN IMPORTANT ENDEAVOR?

The world continues to change, and as it does, the number of people around the globe who are secular continues to grow. In fact, with the rise of the "Nones" (those unaffiliated with any organized religion, especially for the purpose of polling), we are even seeing the growth of nations, such as some of the Scandinavian countries, by and through secular law, living out their cultural identities, values, mores, and laws firmly in the realm of secular humanism.

For each person we had the great pleasure of interviewing, there are millions more who live quiet lives and whose personal experiences make them humanists. Secular activists who choose to help others come from different socioeconomic and educational backgrounds; from different ethnic, racial and national origin groups; and from every age, gender, and sexual preference category. The documentation of these contributions is critical to set the record straight and highlight the efforts of the humanists and nonbelievers who shape our world through their activist lives. Those who are faithless can indeed have strong ethics and finely tuned moral compasses.

Polemicist and writer Christopher Hitchens would often say that religion and spirituality were each part of humanity's first attempt at understanding the nature of the universe and getting at some universal truth.[9] But as we learned from these interviews, these activists put their trust in humanity before the spirit world.

Because god does not exist for activist nonbelievers, all which is planned, designed, and acted upon is driven by rational thought and evidence-based approaches. The consensus of the people we interviewed indicates a high acceptance of human works of literature, mathematics, astronomy, biology, chemistry, and a host of social and physical sciences, which they use to inform their world and to give it purpose, meaning, and understanding. This is the mindset of the individuals in this book. They were "called" to make a difference not through the priesthood but through secular good works; they help make the world a better place and do it for the sake of helping others.

Of course many religious people do find peace and work for peace through their beliefs, and such work must be acknowledged. Many have helped and even have died to make the world a better and safer place because of what their faith has taught them.

In fact, as you'll see in Chapter 1, Marieke Heikens from Holland makes no distinction between religious and secular activism. But the stories of religious good works have already been well-documented. It is time to document the work of nonbelievers who serve the poor, who get witches released from jails, who rehabilitate temple prostitutes, who fight for freedom for those who don't have it, who fight for the victims of sexual abuse, who help rehabilitate prisoners, who help rebuild communities, who sacrifice their lives in the military—and who in fact do what many religious people do; they reach out to the less fortunate with their time and their resources. And if you think about it, why would atheists treat those in need any differently than believers do?

And the power of telling stories about real people and their lives is in the width and depth: the wider community can both lead and learn by example and the moral and emotional depth of nonbelievers is highlighted, showing that nontheists can be (and are) selfless, truly thinking about another's plight and acting on behalf of others without having faith or belief in a personal god.

We have been honored by these participants, who reached down deeply into themselves to help us understand their causes and their journeys. Their help in contextualizing those journeys, both historically and culturally, was fascinating and important.

It is our hope that as you read through their stories you learn about a range of injustices in the world, and that you are as moved as we are by some of the extraordinary humanitarian efforts of our interviewees. We hope you will weep, as we did, in knowing that such courageous, generous, and empathic people grace our world.

PART ONE

Stories have power. They delight, enchant, touch, teach, recall, inspire, motivate, challenge. They help us understand. They imprint a picture on our minds. Consequently, stories often pack more punch than sermons.

–AUTHOR JANET LITHERLAND

....

CHAPTER 1

GODLESS GRACE

Twenty-five of the 192 countries recognized by the United Nations[10] are represented in this chapter, with an additional three profiles of activists who work internationally. We have tried to represent a variety of countries, cultures, classes, ages, and prior religious backgrounds (or lack thereof) to create a snapshot, a kind of global mosaic for our increasingly interconnected world.

We solicited over 100 humanitarian atheists through Facebook, word-of-mouth requests, referrals, and internet searches. Although not every person solicited chose to participate, the overwhelming consensus from all those contacted was a resounding interest in seeing humanist and humanitarian stories in print. The respondents who seemed most appropriate were sent a list of twenty-one questions. The actual interviews, however, did not focus only on those questions. The interviews were conducted via Skype, telephone, or in person. They were free-flowing, varying in length between 35 and 120 minutes, and satisfying beyond anticipation.

....

CYPRUS

MICHAEL ARISTIDOU

IT MAY SEEM like a strange way to begin a chapter on atheist humanitarians, but after speaking with Michael Aristidou, a Greek Cypriot and former Atheist Alliance International board member, we decided it was essential to open with the crucial distinction he made between atheism and humanism: "There is no moral imperative as an atheist to be good!" There are prescriptions in religions for moral behavior that nonbwelievers are not bound to. If an atheist contributes to the wellbeing of others, he does so because he is prompted internally, not for a gain in or fear of an afterlife or acknowledgement from his community. And conversely, if an atheist behaves badly, the spirit world plays no part in unleashing those demons.

Michael is a tireless supporter of human rights and often speaks in Europe and across the United States on issues that impact civil liberties, gay rights, and the importance of secular reasoning in our educational systems and in our laws.

Michael reminds us that "[atheists] are the least trusted people." The intent of this chapter is simply to acquaint the reader with people who "love thy neighbor" and care deeply about others without belief in a deity. This is our attempt to humanize atheists, to prompt believers of all stripes to be willing to reexamine their lack of trust in us. We atheists are indeed gaining in numbers. The time has come to try to get to know us.

·········

PANAMA

HAYDEE MENDEZ

IT WAS 1946 in the Republic of Panama when women finally won the right to vote. Haydee Mendez's mother, the first female dentist in Panama, was one of the Panamanian feminists responsible for making that happen. She died at the age of ninety-eight. On the other hand, her father, still alive at one hundred, is as Haydee describes, "old-fashioned, of course."

Haydee was raised in a Catholic home, became a lawyer, married an engineer, and had four children. She and her husband raised their children as Catholics. They were even somewhat active in their church, teaching Pre-Cana classes to Catholic couples about to get married.

In the nineties, Haydee and her husband "started to read, think, and talk about church dogmas and concluded that it was mythology." (Matthew Alper's book *The "God" Part of The Brain: A Scientific Interpretation of Human Spirituality and God* was the book that influenced them most.)

"We ended up nonbelievers," she told us.

Of their four sons, today, two are believers and two are not.

In 2007, the couple stopped working and moved to the interior of Panama to live out their retirement dreams. For Haydee, that dream was to honor and continue the work of her mother by helping women. She returned to school and earned her PhD in gender and criminal law.

Her work of the last seven years has "fulfilled a lifelong dream" of advancing justice for women. She drafted the bill for the recently approved law against femicide and violence toward women in Panama. She co-wrote *Sexual Harassment: A Labor Problem*, which is the first full-length Panamanian book on sexual harassment.

Haydee and her husband have evolved, and they have evolved together in a union of respect and love that has empowered expansion and change in each of them. The beautiful vibrancy in their lifelong relationship is, indeed, one of life's grace notes.

·········

ISRAEL

GILA SVIRSKY

GILA SVIRSKY, AGE sixty-seven, spends a lot of time trying to "get Israel to behave," as she calls it. As part of the Women's Peace Movement, she has done her share of protesting—sitting in front of bulldozers in an attempt to stop them from demolishing the homes of Palestinians.

The movement is a mix of younger and older women, with several in their nineties who are still willing to chain themselves to trees in the Palestinian territories. For over thirty years, Gila has been working on behalf of women's rights and gay rights in Israel and pushing to end human violations being carried out on the Palestinians in the occupied territories. It is no surprise that she has been jailed on several occasions.

Gila was raised on a chicken farm in New Jersey, attending Orthodox Jewish schools and camps. As a teenager, she read Bertrand Russell's essay "Why I Am Not a Christian," which fueled her growing belief that "God was an invention of people." In college, however, she "came under the influence of an ultra-Orthodox Hasidic rabbi" who encouraged her to set aside her doubts and abide by the principle that "we shall practice our religion and the faith will come." After college, she relocated to Jerusalem, and by age thirty, had given up on "getting to faith."

Gila is a "proud member of the Jewish community" but does not believe in God. Once a year, on Yom Kippur, she attends services at a synagogue but does not pray. The sense of community nourishes her, and she feels lucky to have found a rabbi who speaks meaningfully about "moral principles."

There is a gentleness to Gila which belies her activism. A translator, devoted mother, grandmother, partner, and a lifelong activist for justice and equal rights, Gila embodies *lovingkindness*.

·········

MOROCCO
KACEM EL GAZZALI

KACEM EL GAZZALI claims to be the first atheist to "come out" in Morocco. It was a brave act, but Kacem does not see himself so much as brave but as simply "doing what [he has] to do." When you speak with Kacem, you feel you are talking to a much older man, not only because of his mature voice, but because he exudes wisdom far beyond his twenty-three years.

Kacem grew up in a Muslim family in a small village in Morocco. He attended public school as a young boy, and his family was not as religious as some others: "The Qu'ran was on display in the living room but never opened," he told us.

As early as age eight, he questioned his mother, asking her, "Where is Allah?" Her eyes moved upward as she answered, "Somewhere above us," adding that Kacem "must be good or will burn in hell." This answer caused Kacem to begin to feel uncomfortable, "like a hidden camera was watching [him]."

At age ten, his family relocated to Libya because of "family troubles," and his father became very protective because he feared that Kacem would "fall under the wrong influence" if allowed to play with the other children. His father enrolled Kacem in a moderate Qu'ranic after-school program, where he learned to memorize the Qu'ran.

Then, by the time the family returned to Morocco, Kacem was a teenager and he had fallen behind the curriculum in the Moroccan state school, partially because French was not spoken in Libya. His father thought the easiest way to rectify this problem was to enroll him in an Islamic boarding school, where he would study to be an imam. Now he had entered the world of "hardcore" Islam, the "Saudi Arabian interpretation of religion," as Kacem described it. The students were kept awake, sometimes from three in the morning until midnight, to pray. "The food was terrible," he said, and he could only go home to his family once or twice a month. He had to wear what he calls "Taliban pajamas," and he was "trapped and alone in this extremist world without even a belief in God!"

After this dark year, he became ill with anemia and was sent home to regain his strength. The Kacem who returned home was angry and jealous, one who resented the other teenagers wearing "beautiful jeans." Seeing the change in Kacem, his father allowed him to remain home and return to the state school, but the transition back to moderate life was its own kind of "nightmare." In self-hatred, he would bang his head against the wall and think, "What is wrong with me? I don't believe in Allah," until at school he was exposed to "The Universal Declaration of Human Rights." A pivotal moment, he knew his "new religion" was human rights. Since then he has devoted his life to inspiring others to that end.

Kacem now works in Geneva with the Human Rights Council, having been granted political asylum by Switzerland. He works for freedom of thought and freedom of speech. He is a blogger and an author for the Arab world.

"Atheism is not enough," Kacem said, emphasizing that, "Humanism is what is necessary. It is our moral duty to support each other, to contribute to life, to make a beautiful picture from all the different parts of humanity." Kacem is one of those people who is helping to create this beautiful picture.

....

INDIA

DR. VIJAYAM

A "BORN ATHEIST," Dr. Goparaju Vijayam, age seventy-seven, is the second child of Gora and Saraswathi Gora, and he lives Gandhism (as did his father who wrote a book about his conversations with Gandhi: *An Atheist With Gandhi).*

As a political scientist working for social change, Vijayam is living proof that a life devoted to secular social change and "rationalism" can be a very exciting one. Traveling both nationally and internationally to study, present papers, and participate in conferences, his accomplishments, publications, and honors are staggering. He attended the Martin Luther King School for Social Change at its inception in 1968. He was also a research scholar at the Center for Nonviolent Conflict Resolution in the United States. Additionally, he also served a Director of Research at the Gandhi Peace Foundation for five years. He is also a member of the Pollution Control Board in Vijayawada.

Dr. Vijayam currently serves as the executive director of the Atheist Center of India, which was founded by his parents in 1940. At the Atheist Centre, which is located in Vijayawada, India, "all of [its] people live in community and work together promoting atheism as a positive way of life," he says. The center rehabilitates *Jogins,* or *devadasis,* women who are forced to become sex workers in the name of religion. The center also "rehabilitates women victims of torture" and works toward "castelessness [and the] eradication of Indian untouchability."

Currently, science and scientific education are perhaps Dr. Vijayam's most pressing priorities. The Centre has received national attention for its investigations of the "paranormal, witchcraft and sorcery in hundreds of villages." They are also "striving hard to start an Atheist University which would help to do in-depth research from around the world on how atheists, rationalists, freethinkers, and skeptics have contributed, through reform and movement, to the society."

"Hinduism is not opposed to evolution," Dr. Vijayam explained. In fact, the Government of India released a postage stamp with Charles Darwin on it. The *Charvaka* (aka *Lokāyata*) school of philosophy—Indian materialism—flatly denied the existence of gods. The *Charvaka* system only believed in the four classic elements: earth, water, fire, and air. Ancient India, as he classifies it, "is not only a cradle land of religion, but also of atheism.... they challenged the authority of the *Vedas* (scriptures) and the *Upanishads*." The concept of karma, rebirth, and the soul were not accepted by early Indian atheists. It was "the later advocates of the Nyaya and Vaisheshika systems [that] imported God into them."

India, with its multicultural, multi-religious, and multi-ethnic makeup; its ancient godless roots; and its embrace of Charles Darwin, is fertile soil for atheism. In fact, Dr. Vijayam believes that "the twenty-first century is the century of atheism and humanism." He quotes the words of Buddha: "When you find that anything agrees with reason and is conducive to the good and benefit of one and all, then accept it and live up to it." It is fitting that "*Jai Insaan*," which means "Victory to Humans" in Hindi, is the Atheist Centre's motto.

....

BANGLADESH
TASLIMA NASRIN

AT FOURTEEN, the waif-like Taslima Nasrin heard a song about Bengali revolutionary Khudiram Bose and said to herself, "I want to be brave like him." Then she made that happen. From a northern town in East Pakistan (now Bangladesh) to global recognition, Taslima has soldiered on with what could only be called astounding bravery. She has faced *fatwas* and threats of beheading and been placed in safe houses and exiles in order to expose the atrocities of the fundamentalist Muslim world.

Taslima started her career as a gynecologist who worked in Bangladesh clinics. She witnessed the effect of the patriarchal system that enforced women's objectification, as informed by Islamic *hadiths* (the teachings of Muhammad), on women's healthcare and became a staunch feminist.

She was also influenced by her mother. Taslima's first memoir, *Meyebela, My Bengali Girlhood* is dedicated to her mother, "who suffered all her life." Her mother was a devout Muslim woman who married to an abusive, philandering physician with no use for religion. Taslima took the best of both worlds: her mother's early nurturing and her father's scientific reasoning and obsessive devotion to education. But her parents were only part of what formed her; she grew up surrounded by violence, poverty, starvation, rioting, and guerrilla warfare. She witnessed the devastating horrors that befell not only her own family, but their servants, friends, neighbors, and relatives. Meanwhile, her mother told her the cause of their suffering was the *jinn*, an evil wind, and could only beseech *Allah* to save them.

Taslima has lived in exile since 1993, taking up residence in several countries along the way. During a recent spate of atheist murders in Bangladesh, Taslima fled from India to North America. Now an accomplished poet and author, she has written over forty books that have been translated into thirty languages and counting. Her accomplishments and her awards are too numerous to mention, but some of note are the Feminist of the Year Award and the International Humanist Award, granted by the International Humanist and Ethical Union. She spoke at the Reason Rally in Washington, DC, in 2012.

Years ago, singer/songwriter Joan Baez wrote "Song of Bangladesh" in which she calls out, "Once again we stand aside...see a teenage mother's vacant eyes." Taslima Nasrin, seeing through her own mother's eyes and the eyes of countless other women, did not stand aside. She has graced the world with her vision and her bravery.

....

PHILIPPINES

RED TANI

THE FILIPINO FREETHINKERS won a Globe Telecom award in 2011 for being the most influential trendsetter with their website "that shaped opinion, moved people, and prompted action." In a country that is 80 percent Catholic and where abortion is illegal, a *secular* organization received this digital honor. Red Tani, the organization's founder, attributes this to two primary factors: (1) Although theirs is a predominantly Catholic country, Filipinos are "not fundamentalists," and (2) Filipino Freethinkers is allied worldwide with non-atheist groups in their fight for women's rights. Recently, they have expanded their alliance internationally and joined with Catholics for Choice in that struggle.

Filipino Freethinkers has unexpectedly exploded, along with the growing acceptance of atheism in the Philippines, where Catholicism is so culturally ingrained that Red never had any exposure to information that would have helped him consider atheism "a reasonable choice" until age twenty-two—and that happened accidentally. Having graduated from all-Catholic schools, including a Catholic college, Red found himself with a job that allowed him a lot of free time. Since he "couldn't play video games at work," he explained, he read eBooks, beginning with Dan Brown's *The Da Vinci Code*. There he read that certain rites in Catholicism were borrowed from paganism, and he followed that trail all the way to Robert Ingersoll and Bertrand Russell. By age twenty-five, he was a nonbeliever, and he was lonely in a country of believers.

He began Filipino Freethinkers in order to have a community. This was a modest beginning to a viral success story. In 2012, the organization fought the Catholic Church in its opposition to the Reproductive Health Bill which would allow sex education and contraception in the Philippines. His organization also currently fights for the rights of the Filipino LGBTQ community.

Politically speaking, Red is an anarchist who does not want the government controlling his personal life. He and his partner of ten years, a Filipino woman of Chinese origin, promised themselves to each other in a ceremony that they designed themselves. "It was quite romantic," he said with a chuckle.

In 2012, Red was invited to appear on a popular Filipino talk show, Boy Abunda's *The Bottom Line.* The episode was titled "Discover the Life Without a God." Red spoke about the burden he felt "of representing atheists in [his] country." It was a home run— one of the most successful of Boy Abunda's interviews according to the show's producers. Red smiled as he told us, "People saw atheists could be nice people. People just haven't been exposed to atheism."

It is an amazing journey. Red, this electronics and communications engineer, graduate of a Benedictine University, and lover of video games, who may not have set out to change the world is, in fact, doing just that.

·····.·····

CUBA

ALBERTO ROQUE GUERRA

IN A POOR COUNTRY where the first drop of a forty-three dollar bottle of rum is tossed into the sink to honor *orishas* (the Santerían gods), Alberto Roque Guerra is an atheist.

When Fidel Castro took power in 1959, Cuba was declared a secular country by constitutional law. He deported any priests who were not Cuban. Nonetheless, he left the churches intact, albeit closed. Since then, state strictures on religion have been relaxed in Cuba and it is thought that more than 60 percent of the population has been baptized and identifies as Catholic.

Both Popes John Paul II and Benedict XVI have visited Cuba, and the country eagerly prepared for Pope Francis's visit in September of 2015. However, during the many years of enforced secularization, it is likely that people continued to honor their orishas privately at home. The religious situation in Cuba, in short, is complicated and changing rapidly.

Even before the Cuban Revolution, Alberto's grandfather was a nonbeliever. Alberto was raised in a poor, rural, secular home that was full of "generosity and community cooperation." Born in 1969, Alberto was the oldest of three children and until the age of eleven lived in Guanamon de Armenteros, a sugarcane-producing district. When his father was a child, he had to sell avocados on the side of the road to provide for his grandparents. However, after a "transformation in the countryside" in the 1970s, his father joined a "farming cooperative," functioning as a mechanic for the repair of the farm machinery.

There was never a moment when Alberto wasn't moved to help others: "To be useful to other people is central to my life," he said. Alberto's family lived on higher land than some of the other families, and during the inevitable flooding that would result during the hurricanes, other families would sleep at his home. "In the seventies," he said, "solidarity was very strong in the humble countryside."

As part of the literacy campaign in Cuba, the four students with the best grades from each district were chosen to go to Vladimir Ilich Lenin Vocational School, a boarding school in Havana.

Four thousand of Cuba's best and brightest youth were chosen to study there, including Alberto. He refers to this as "the brilliant moment" in his life.

Now, he is a doctor of Internal Medicine working in Intensive Care at Freyre de Andrade General Hospital in Havana. He is also a human rights activist. In 2009, Alberto graduated from the Equitas International Centre for Human Rights Education in Montreal. He also serves as part of the gender team for sex reassignment surgeries at CENESEX (the Cuban National Center for Sex Education).

Interestingly enough, Cuba's socialized medical system pays for transgender surgery, but many gay people are still cautious about being publicly demonstrative in Cuba, and there is much more work to be done for the rights of the LGBTQ community there. To that end, Alberto runs informal training groups throughout Cuba and advances the cause through Twitter and his blog *Proqueer*. He lives with Camilo, his partner of seventeen years, in Havana.

If you want to see Alberto in action, watch Michael Moore's documentary *Sicko*. After being turned away from Guantanamo Bay with his boatloads of uninsured ill Americans, Moore took these Americans to a hospital in Havana, and Alberto was one of the physicians on duty who took care of them, without compensation. If not another "brilliant moment" in Alberto's life, it certainly must have been an unexpected one!

·····⁣·····

INTERNATIONAL
MARISSA TORRES LANGSETH

GENEROSITY AND ENERGY emanate from Marissa Torres Langseth, the founding Chairwoman of PATAS (Philippine Atheists and Agnostics) and later HAPI (Humanist Alliance Philippines, International). She is well-suited for her activist "calling" to help Filipinos emerge from abject poverty, poverty which she attributes in large measure to their belief in "imaginary beings" and an after-life. Born the third daughter of eight children into a poor Roman Catholic family in Cebu, she may seem an unlikely future leader of Southeast Asia's emergence from the paradigm of religious thinking.

Marissa dates her early skepticism to the fifth grade when she was introduced to science and became fascinated by it. In third grade, she was already questioning why Santa Claus only brought dolls to the richer girls and not to "poor, but good girls" like her. She felt Santa was a "fairy tale" and began to have doubts about the existence of God as well. An honor student, she eventually went on to study nursing and was sent to Saudi Arabia to work for five years. Loneliness and the need for community almost drove her at one point to convert to Islam. She moved in and out of religion, even being briefly "born again" when she came to the United States. In 1996, she fell in love with an American Protestant and got married in his church in New York City, where they now live.

Then came the terrorist attack of September 11th. As Marissa watched the second tower of the World Trade Center fall, her belief in God was gone forever: "If there was a God, he would have stopped that plane," she explained. She felt that it was "the right time to come out as an atheist," but she quickly lost many friends. People unfriended her on Facebook, she became the "black sheep" of her family, and her marriage was severely strained as a result, with only their "deep love" keeping it from unraveling. Then, she joined the American Humanist Association and met likeminded people. Empowered by feeling less isolated, she went to Manila in 2012 to help finance and organize the first Atheist Convention in Southeast Asia through her new organization PATAS which was, according to Marissa, "history in the making."

She retired from PATAS in 2013 and refers to her involvement in PATAS as her militant period. But the resignation left a hole in her heart, and she reinvented her atheist activism through the creation of the Humanist Alliance Phillipines, International (HAPI), an organization that works with religious groups and aims to build a bridge between secular humanism and religion. It is a gentler organization than PATAS that has attracted many other nurses and humanitarian workers, but like PATAS, they feed the poor and establish libraries to educate people. Darwin is not taught in school in the Philippines.

HAPI also does much to address the issues of the LGBTQ community in the Philippines. One of Marissa's sisters is a lesbian. When her mother discovered this, she tried to have Marissa's sister killed, and her sister had to flee for her life. Though HAPI was only "born" on December 25, 2013 and launched on January 1, 2014, Marissa proudly told us, "As of August 2014, HAPI has more than four thousand members!"

Marissa is a giver. She eventually became a nurse practitioner and practices activism in her everyday life. She currently is sponsoring a seventeen-year-old scholar through his studies. As a nurse, she protects her patients by challenging any doctors who order unnecessary procedures for their own financial gain. She told us that, "Not only do these physicians harm their patients, but [they] deplete the financial resources of Medicare." One doctor has "threatened [her] life two or three times." But Marissa says she "[doesn't] care if they fire me." A firecracker, full of life, Marissa pays it forward.

KENYA

NANCY

NANCY* IS NO STRANGER to violence. After years of legal struggles, the United States government recently granted her political
asylum and she is safer than she's been in a long time. A victim
of election violence in 2007 in Kenya, she was seriously injured
during the upheaval that overtook her nation— an event spurred
by partisan accusations and counteraccusations of "rigging" the
presidential elections. The spontaneous riots that broke out following the highly contested election, which was won by a member
of the *Kikuyu* tribe, brought unspeakable pain and suffering to
those who were "considered to be at the wrong place at the wrong
time." When Nancy thinks of what happened to her, she speaks
of trauma; she "freezes and shudders run down [her] whole body,
and tears start streaming down [her] face" because her life was
forever altered by the aftermath. Nancy is of the *Kalenjin* tribe in
Kenya, and she still isn't sure whether the violence towards her
was random or if she was targeted.

She is also a refugee because of domestic violence. In Kenya,
where reporting of domestic violence is frowned upon, Nancy
reached a point where she could no longer tolerate her husband
"making [her] life hell, to the point of it spilling to the children."
She made the decision to seek help and was consequently ostracized by her society for "going against the norm." There was
another obstacle; in Kenyan tradition, a mother cannot take the
children because "they are always considered the man's property."
Undaunted, Nancy is "fighting back and optimistic about winning
custody of her children."

An ethical humanist and a self-proclaimed "proud atheist,"
Nancy is very disturbed because she believes that "Africans are
going backward" and that the continent is becoming increasingly
religious. The majority of her village is religious. Her grandparents' generation worshipped the sun, *Asis*, but missionaries converted her community to Protestantism. Nancy attributes her lack
of belief in a deity to her father: "My father never mentioned God.

He told us we had to trust in ourselves, that we were our own God, that we control our destinies."

When Nancy's husband mistreated and beat her, her father warned him that there would be consequences. When her husband didn't stop abusing her, Nancy left with nothing but her children and the clothes on their backs. One of Nancy's friends wasn't so brave. She stayed with her husband and "prayed upon the Lord to deliver her from her yoke"—with tragic results. Nancy's friend was murdered at the hands of her husband.

For Nancy, god-belief is disempowering. She adamantly believes that when "you turn over your power to deities," you lose your own power, which is why she is proud of the example she has set for her children to not "accept anyone's crap." "I gave up everything for my children to learn this," she said.

Nancy intends to stop teaching and go back to school to study social work in order to help "people who are voiceless to find a voice [and] to heal, to offer back to society the help [she has] received and to bring sanity back into people's lives."

   * *Nancy, still fearful about revealing her real name, chose this pseudonym because "it was a name for someone who belonged nowhere and everywhere."*

……..….

UNITED STATES

LEE FLEMING

LEE FLEMING, a forty-four-year-old ex-Lutheran from the Bible Belt of America, left his career as a sommelier and restaurant manager to become a paramedic for the New York City Fire Department. The sense of meaning this career change added to his life was worth the significant pay cut; Lee feels strongly that because his desire to help others came from himself and not from fear of punishment or hope of reward in an afterlife, he does his job more purely, consistently, and fully. For Lee, and for many secular humanists, giving out of a sense of duty is hollow and perhaps not personally rewarding: "[Giving back as a nonbeliever] has a very important advantage that should be noted....When people give from their hearts, it is better for both the giver and the receiver," he says.

But he adds, "That is not to say that religious people don't give from their hearts." According to Lee, there is a caveat: "[Religious people] believe if they are good, then good will come to them. And we all know that isn't necessarily true. When people discover that life is indeed not fair, they can resent their generosity—they can become bitter and wish they had lived a more self-centered life."

Lee's journey from the primarily nondrinking, non-dancing, intolerant Southern-Baptist world of Blue Eye, Missouri, to New York City was a gradual one, but nothing less than a transformation of consciousness. It began at age sixteen, after he read Richard Bach's Illusions: *The Adventures of a Reluctant Messiah*, a book recommended by his music teacher. Shortly after, he spent his junior year of high school abroad in Norway. And although much of what he did there was church-related, he gained perspective on the culture he grew up in back home.

As Lee describes, "[I] was able to walk through a doorway that led to nonconformity." He continued that "searching for truth" and exploring ideas that people cling to for comfort, leading him to his atheism. Lee feels comforted by his nonbelief partly because he has surrendered to the idea that we can't control our destinies.

Having replaced his religious values with humanist values, Lee has found himself. He has found his center, his vitality, and he has become more whole. The more whole the self is, the more stable the self is. And the more stable people are, the more stable society is. What could be more important?

....

INTERNATIONAL

SHARIF RAHMAN

SHARIF RAHMAN OPENED a nonprofit organization—operating under the name ASA—to assist disabled people. Cloaked in what he says is necessary secrecy, Sharif does not tell people what the acronym stands for: American Secular Association. In the Indian, Bangladeshi, and Pakistani community in Queens, New York, where Sharif's center is located, his Muslim, Hindu, and Christian clients and employees might "close him down" if they knew he was an atheist.

Sharif says he is "motivated by fear," and soldiers on in his passion both for helping people with disabilities and his passion for atheism. And he is no stranger to fear.

He grew up in what he calls a "liberal Muslim" home. He attended public schools throughout Bangladesh as a young boy. By the age of ten, he began to doubt the existence of God. By high school his family settled in Dhaka where, he attended Notre Dame, a prestigious Catholic secondary school. His family viewed education as being more important than religion. His atheism solidified, and he attended college in Bangladesh, rooming with childhood friends. But when he hung a poster of his hero Taslima Nasrin in his room, his friends kicked him out to the street without his belongings. He never saw them again.

In June 2001, in Dhaka, the capital of Bangladesh, his military father "went to the hospital and never came back." His family, assuming his father had been assassinated, had to separate and hide. At age twenty-one, Sharif left college and in September of that year, he obtained a student visa for the United States.

Four years later he was hit, head-on, by a drunk driver. After staying in a coma for two weeks, he had brain surgery, resulting in two metal plates in his skull and a disability that he says has made his life "a living hell."

At age thirty-three, Sharif married who he thought was a liberal Muslim girl, and they had a daughter. When his daughter was four-years-old, his wife became a "born-again Muslim" who replaced her jeans with the hijab. Though he has since divorced her, the jury is still out on whether his daughter will be indoctrinated as a Muslim.

Sharif has experienced and witnessed the suffering that can result from religious intolerance. And still recently, atheist bloggers have been beaten and killed on the streets and in their homes in Bangladesh by *extremists*. The Prime Minister has recently rejected the Blasphemy Law which demands the death penalty for anyone speaking out against Muhammad. (However, older laws still on the books do call for the jailing and prosecution of those who blaspheme any faith.)

Sharif has achieved his dream of helping the disabled, having opened seven centers in seven states in the US, with more to come, but he is working toward his dream of seeing religious tolerance in the world. That is a dream he understands may be long in coming.

·····•·····

AUSTRALIA

ALICE CARR

ALICE CARR WAS a lonely child. As the only child of divorced parents in a town in the north of England, she had welcomed the comfort of the community her mother had found in a doomsday cult called Brahma Kumaris. But many twists and turns later, at age thirty-eight, Alice is heading a very different kind of community in Melbourne, Australia; she is the president of Progressive Atheists Inc. which has a mission statement opposing "racism, sexism, homophobia, economic-class exploitation, age discrimination."

Alice's journey to atheism began early. A child of joint custody, she spent half of her time with each parent; her mother was a member of Brahma Kumaris, and her father was an atheist. At age six, her mother told her that the world was five thousand years old. When she told her father this, he said, "Who the hell told you that?! The world is 13.7 billion years old, give or take." Even at that age, she liked the "give or take" part and so, the questioning began. At age fifteen, her mother had moved on from Brahma Kumaris, but Alice felt lost and still found structure in the cult.

But life in the cult was not easy. She couldn't lead a life that required celibacy. And waking up at 3:00 AM for meditation seemed unsustainable. Finally, at age twenty-seven, she could no longer tolerate the internal conflict between what she believed and what she wanted to believe. She took a courageous leap to "rationality" and embraced atheism.

The next two years were painful for both her and her religious husband, who she had met while in Brahma Kumaris. When Alice became strident in her rejection of a spiritual life, her husband accused her of "spiritual abuse." It was only because of their extremely strong bond that the relationship survived her exit from religion. Two years later, he became an atheist himself.

Freedom from false belief is very important to Alice. During our interview, some of her four children played in the background. She asked two of them, ages seven and four, whether or not they believed in God; the older one said yes, the younger said no, preferring to agree with his twelve-year-old brother. She told us she would feel like a failure if any of her children grew up tyrannized by belief in a deity: "If they felt guilty for having sex or were hampered by superstitious belief, I would have failed them—failed at making them feel safe without religion, leading to lives based on a false premise."

Alice also spoke emotionally about losing a baby boy at seventeen weeks. Though she delivered at home, when grief struck, she went to the hospital to attend a support group with some dozen other mothers who had lost a child. Many of those mothers referred to their children as "angels now."

She realized that she had a sense of closure that many of the religious moms didn't have. The mothers who saw their babies in heaven seemed almost haunted by them: "When your child dies it's the guilt—what did I do wrong? Belief in god seems to imply that you or the child in some way deserved to be punished—of course it's just a tragic loss."

I asked Alice if she was afraid of her own death. She unhesitatingly responded, "Terrified!" and confessed that after her spiritual period, it was hardest to let go of her belief in reincarnation and nirvana because those beliefs took away her fear of death. Now, when she wakes up in the middle of the night and thinks of her mortality, she engages her community on Facebook or watches *Star Trek* to escape the anxious thoughts.

The organization she heads, Progressive Atheists Inc., has thirty-one humanitarian agenda items, too numerous to mention here. Their most recent effort addresses the church cover-up of child abuse by priests, brothers, and nuns. Lawyer Judy Courtin, invited as a speaker for an event in 2013 spoke on "The Royal Commission into Child Sexual Abuse," explaining the inadequacies of the laws in Australia that enable such horrendous abuses of children. And because there is no legal separation of church and state in Australia, Australia has uniquely complicated legal challenges to address among other issues.

Alice volunteers up to fifty hours a week while raising her four kids, partially crediting the cult in which she was raised with an anti-materialistic value system that still motivates her for the greater good.

Brava to Alice Carr. Her brain won over her emotions. She relinquished comfort for rationalism, and she didn't throw out the good with the bad. She kept the humanitarian, community values from the cult and gave up the storyline that no longer made sense to her. She may no longer sleep as peacefully but in her waking hours, she is no longer living with cognitive dissonance. She is whole.

....

UNITED STATES
ZOLTAN ISTVAN

ZOLTAN ISTVAN LOVES life, and he would like to live forever. He's packed enough living into his forty-two years to make most people tired (if you google Zoltan, you might find him volcano boarding on YouTube). But as he sees it, he's just beginning.

Originally sent to Kashmir on assignment by *National Geographic*, Zoltan became familiar with the longest war in history, a war between Pakistan and India, a war between countries with nuclear weapons, a war between Muslims and Hindus. Traveling as a Hungarian journalist has allowed him entry and accessibility to countries and people American journalists are denied. Out of that story grew his full-length, award-winning documentary *Pawns of Paradise* that exposes the devastating plight of the millions of refugees in Kashmir—a paradise lost indeed.

Zoltan also served for four years as the director of WildAid, an international conservation group that works to stop the billion-dollar illegal wildlife trade in Southeast Asia. Zoltan grew up Catholic in America. In 1968, his parents escaped illegally with him in stow from Hungary in a hay truck, leaving his small sister with her grandparents until they could bring her to the United States. He studied at Columbia University under Robert Thurman, majoring in philosophy and religious studies. As part of his studies, Zoltan had to read the entire Old Testament and New Testament in order to know scripture by heart. When he closed the "book," he "simply didn't have any more belief," he told us.

Then, when 9/11 happened, he told us his atheist "activism rose up," because if there were "no religion, no planes would have flown into the Twin Towers."

Zoltan the humanitarian, the husband, the father, the journalist, the filmmaker, the novelist and the philosopher is also a visionary and a futurist. He is a transhumanist who believes that science and technology will save people his age and younger from death. Zoltan sees atheism as "a natural bridge" to transhumanism. And without a belief in the hereafter, it's reasonable he would definitely want to extend his stay.

While covering a story of Vietnamese farmers who dig up unexploded land mines for a dollar a day, Zoltan almost stepped on a mine, and in that moment mortality became real. It's interesting to ponder how one's values and desires might be altered if we thought we were going to live beyond our current lifespans: would we still choose to live a moral life and for how long? Regardless of whether he signs up for the extended bionic stay, Zoltan's getting it all in anyway.

....

UNITED KINGDOM

SUE COX

WHEN TRAGEDY BEARS down on a person, it can leave them broken—or transformed. But as it turns out, Sue Cox is strong at the broken places. In 1988, Sue's nineteen-year-old son Nicholas died in a car crash. She was swallowed by grief and wanted to die. When she climbed her way out of that loss, she emerged an atheist.

Sue was raised in a "fiercely Catholic" home in Lincolnshire, a small, isolated seaside town. The impact of Catholicism on Sue was abject fear: "I had a sense of being watched [by God]," she said. She was told to pray to God and "offer up her suffering to pay for her sins."

During her tween years, a priest moved into the family home, joining her mother, her two spinster aunts, and her ailing father. During those years, this priest sexually abused and raped Sue on multiple occasions. When Sue's mother found out, she did nothing, "not even changing the sheets." Sue told us that her mother would say, "It's part of God's plan."

At the age of seventeen, Sue finally ran away from home. She self-harmed, developed an eating disorder, drank, and fell into an abusive marriage. She felt "like an alien...vermin...in a world [she] was estranged from."

At age twenty-nine, in 1976, with the help of Alcoholics Anonymous, she became sober and "the veils" began to lift. Two years later, she left her husband with six children under the age of twelve in tow. She learned to drive, went back to school, and began to trust in herself. She also began to reexamine her beliefs. "Atheism grew on me...[it was] an organic process."

Twenty-five years ago, she remarried an atheist. Her remaining children and grandchildren are sources of joy and pride to her. She is now actively helping others as a psychotherapist alongside one of her daughters who helps in her work. Sue considers this work improving the lives of others to be her privilege and "absolute passion."

Sue has taught 13,000 professionals and counting in the neuroscience of addiction and written a book on the topic titled *Auricular Acupuncture and Addiction*. She travels around England to all of its 128 maximum-security prisons, where she teaches designated prison officers about the neuroscience of addiction in an effort to improve the quality of life for both "lifers," who have life sentences, and other prisoners. "Britain's prison system is quite compassionate," Sue finds, and she adds to that compassion. Having developed a formula that can improve people's lives, she also teaches healthcare workers throughout England's healthcare system.

In 2010, Sue traveled from her home in the Midlands to London to receive a Lifetime Achievement Award awarded by the Royal College of Medicine for her work in addiction. This happened to coincided with Pope Benedict XVI's visit to England. Twenty-thousand people congregated in London to protest the Vatican's protection of pedophile priests, and Sue serendipitously found herself on the back of a truck speaking out for the first time about her experience with clergy rape in her youth.

Finally, she felt her isolation lift, and at sixty-two, she said she "felt like part of the human race" for the first time. This experience inspired her to form her charity Survivors Voice Europe, which she began with her cofounder and fellow clergy rape survivor, Tom Leer, from the Netherlands. Survivors Voice Europe helps victims become victors by helping people speak out and heal.

In 2014, Sue received the Inspirational Woman of the Year award from Inspiration Awards for Women for her human rights work. Martin Luther King, Jr. said, "Our lives begin to end the day we become silent about things that matter." Through sharing her story, Sue Cox became empowered and her "labor of love" is now empowering others.

⋯⋯

UNITED STATES
CONOR ROBINSON

CONOR ROBINSON CAME by his humanitarianism honestly. His father is a nurse practitioner, and his mother is a marriage and family therapist who worked in child protective services. His atheism was harder won, however. Conor grew up going regularly to a nondenominational Christian church, but didn't "feel" his parents were truly religious. By age ten, Conor was debating the existence of God with his "emotionally volatile" father. He told us his father's "failure to present good arguments" moved him from doubt and agnosticism to complete nonbelief. He still believes that his father's need for church stems more from his need for community and acceptance in that community than from religious conviction.

Conor grew up in a rural northern California "cow town" that he describes as "conservative, racist, sexist, and homophobic." Feeling isolated in high school, Conor decided to apply to Yale University, where he expected to find other atheists like himself. When he got there, he discovered more "religious groups and a capella groups," motivating him to form the Yale Humanist Society. What began for Conor as a "political maneuver" turned into a life path as a humanist once he discovered "the power of service...the power of shared work as a basis of trust."

After graduating from Yale, Conor returned to his home state of California to work for Teach For America where he was assigned to teach special education students in East Los Angeles. The tricky waters of collaborating with other inner-city teachers developed in him a passion, as well as a skillset, that was excellent preparation for his next undertaking.

In 2012, at age twenty-four, Conor established the Pathfinders Project. He and three other humanists spent a year travelling the world to perform service work supporting clean water initiatives, education, human rights, and environmental conservation in Africa, Asia, and Latin America. At the time of the interview, the four humanists had just set up camp in Isla Puná, arriving after a latrine building endeavor in Haiti, to join Water Ecuador in building their seventh Water Center there.

The Pathfinders Project, sponsored by Foundation Beyond Belief, established the Humanist Service Corps upon the group's return. Conor's hope is that this shared "boots on the ground" approach will contribute to a more positive view of atheists and help to build relationships between secular humanist volunteers and the religious humanitarians they are volunteering with.

Conor had gone searching for a community of likeminded people and instead he ended up creating one. Conor's father had wanted his son to believe in the existence of God but now finds himself the proud dad of an atheist, activist son. In fact, a few months after this interview, Conor's father declared himself a "full-fledged humanist with all the rights, privileges, benefits, and yes, responsibilities appertaining to this," rejecting "the notion of a rescuing deity"—a change in belief for which he thanks his "wonderful son, who led [him] to this place, without ever judging [him]." To Conor, he says, "I love you, Little Hero. Come home soon."

Those are the beautiful turns of life—if we can just manage to leave our hearts and minds open.

....

NIGERIA
LEO IGWE

LEO IGWE, ONE of five children, was born in a village in southeast Nigeria to Catholic parents. His father was headmaster at a local Catholic primary school. And his mother took care of the family, having attended less than two years of school.

Leo was not a privileged child groomed to devote his life to activism—and certainly not an atheist. He was sent to a seminary at age twelve to get an education. After nine years, he read Bertrand Russell's essay "Why I Am Not a Christian," which began a three-year process of rethinking his views on religion that eventually resulted in his departure from the seminary—and the starting of a new life as a humanitarian atheist.

His family thought it was a phase that he'd quickly outgrow when he faced the real world and discovered how impossible it was to change the powers that be. He was twenty-four years old. His father told his mother, "Let the boy hit his head against the wall a few times and he'll see." But even Leo's parents misjudged his conviction. He's now forty-four and still undaunted. He puts one foot in front of the other and is unstoppable.

Sometimes, he's astonished at his own results. In 2010, he received a letter from an Australia entity requesting that he embark on a speaking tour across their country. "A speaking tour, I thought. What is a speaking tour? Who would want me to speak and about what? English is my second language. I'm not even good looking. For what? I was so nervous from the time I got that letter, I can't tell you," he said. But Leo did have things to say. He spoke about the time he traveled to Malawi and slowly coaxed atheist activist George Thindwa to courageously expose the unlawful imprisonment of fifty women who had been accused of being witches, resulting in their release from jail. In his work against what he describes as "harmful traditional beliefs" like ritual killings and other atrocities, Leo chips away at the irrationality of the thinking behind such beliefs. He raises money to support and rescue the orphans of the women who had been killed or maimed by witch hunters, orphans who had been abandoned and deemed untouchable because locals were afraid of being drawn into "the devil's world." Leo also speaks out against the caste system because as he explains, "the people born into lower castes have no hope of rising above virtual slavery." He also is working for the acceptance of gay marriage.

The span of Leo's empathy, his rationalism, and his activism is wide, and he has paid a huge price for that activism. He has been beaten, robbed, and sued, and his family has been attacked. His father was beaten so badly that one of his eyes had to be removed.

When we asked Leo whether he thought people were basically good or bad, he said they could be both. He strongly believes that what turns a person in one direction or the other is their beliefs, and he strongly believes that Christianity and Islam reinforce the legitimacy of practices like ritual killings. He cites Abraham being commanded by God to sacrifice his son as an example: "A deity somewhere is gratified by the killing and gives a spiritual reward to the killer in the hereafter."

When we spoke, Leo was studying in southern Germany before doing his fieldwork in the witch camps of Ghana. It's the biblical mandate from Exodus 22:18—"Suffer not a witch to live"—that drives these Pentecostals to believe that evil can be carried by certain people. People also dismember hunchbacks because they are believed to contain a substance that can make people rich.

We asked Leo if he was inspired by Nelson Mandela because he seemed so willing to sacrifice his own life and pleasures for his ideals. He told us: "Whenever things got too dangerous and it seemed I might lose my life or the cause I was fighting for would come to nothing, I drew strength from the story of Nelson Mandela."

We were left in tears of awe after his story and grateful that people such as Leo exist, wondering what magical combination of life experiences help to build character like that of Leo Igwe and if we knew, how could we reproduce that combination.

IRAN / UNITED KINGDOM
MARYAM NAMAZIE

WHEN YOU SPEAK to Maryam Namazie, it's obvious that she was raised with love and support. Gentleness and humility are at the center of her philosophy and of her political activism, the core of which is to "defend people's right to be free from fear."

Before her family had to "flee across the world" in response to the Islamic republic formed after the Iranian Revolution of 1979, Maryam was raised in Tehran, Iran. Her grandfather was an Islamic scholar. Her mother converted to Islam (from Protestantism) when she married Maryam's father. As a Muslim, her father prays five times a day. He doesn't drink, gamble or eat pork, and he is proud of his well-known atheist, activist daughter—even though he cannot visit Iran, even though his daughter is on a blacklist, and even though his own father "is turning in his grave."

Maryam's grave concern is for people who are "crushed under the boot of political Islam." In response to the death penalty for apostates under sharia law, she started the Council of Ex-Muslims to challenge Islamism and break the taboo that comes with leaving Islam and becoming an atheist.

In response to the sharia courts in the United Kingdom that adjudicate family matters for many Muslims, she began One Law for All, a movement to dismantle parallel legal systems. She also responded by becoming spokesperson for Iran Solidarity, Equal Rights Now, and Fitnah-Movement for Women's Liberation.

During the Danish cartoon crisis, she stepped up as one of the twelve signers of *A Manifesto Against Islamism*, which called radical Muslim belief a danger to world peace: "the world now faces a new totalitarian threat: Islamism."

She has pushed for international solidarity through her extensive refugee rights work in more than twenty countries, including Ethiopian refugees in the Sudan and Iranian refugees in Turkey. She was also formerly the executive director of the International Federation of Iranian Refugees for many years. Though her other humanitarian work is too extensive to list, it all revolves around one central theme: the equal right of all people to coexist without fear.

Maryam currently lives in London with her husband and nine-year-old son who attends a state school there. As a nonbeliever, raising a child can be a challenge when religion is often taught as truth, and she often feels "forced to talk about religion" with her son in an effort to counter the message given at school where "religion is imposed" on him. Her son has decided that he does not believe in God, but feels such intense pressure to believe that he conceals his lack of belief from his friends. In her maternal protectiveness, Maryam has a little case of "religion envy": if only she could offer the comfort of eternal life to her son when he asks what will happen after death. Such is the struggle between wrapping our loved ones in warm blankets and speaking our truth to them. But she speaks the truth, as she sees it, to the world, and that is the temple her son has the privilege of growing up in.

⋯⋯⋯

ARGENTINA

FERNANDO ESTEBAN LOZADA

FERNANDO ESTEBAN LOZADA considers atheism a part of his identity. Though he was raised in a majority Catholic country by Catholic parents who made sure he received all the Catholic sacraments and educated in Catholic schools until the age of eighteen, Fernando was never comfortable with the notion of "suffering being rewarded," which was the "moral basis of Christianity" as he learned it. During adolescence, he read Nietzsche and "felt liberated" because he realized "it was possible to live without suffering, to be completely happy and a good person without religion." "I was an atheist and didn't know it," he said.

Now, age forty-one, Fernando is helping atheists to "cease to feel like foreigners in their own country." Founder of Atheists of Mar del Plata (*Ateos Mar del Plata*), he created and organized the First National Congress of Atheism in Argentina in 2008. He then became president of the next three congresses. He became the appointed spokesperson for the Latin America of the International Freethought Association (*Asociación Internacional de Libre Pensamiento*), which organized the "First March Toward a Secular State," and most notably presented a complaint at the Argentinian National Institute Against Discrimination (*Instituto Nacionalcontra la Discriminación, la Xenofobia y el Racismo*, INADI) directed at a communication written by Pope Francis in which he had encouraged "the fight against atheism." INADI did in fact determine that the pope's text was discriminatory!

As a mechanical engineer, he is part of a team that develops biomedical implants to replace joints and to repair tendons. As a citizen, he joins forces with religious people to build a "better society," fighting against fascism and racism and for the legalization of abortion and LGBTQ rights.

For Fernando, his atheism and his humanitarian contributions are inseparable. "When I broke prejudices, pre-concepts and taboos, I could see the world more clearly," he said. "In this way the impulse to help people who were oppressed by social mandates was born in me. I wanted everyone to have the opportunity to build their consciences so they could live without fear and guilt." Because Fernando believes atheism gave him the "freedom to think and feel," he tells us that he "became a stronger and more responsible citizen."

·····.·····

IRELAND

MICHAEL NUGENT

FIFTY-FIVE YEAR old Michael Nugent is a comedy writer, but he finds nothing funny about terrorism. In his anti-terrorism work in Ireland, he "campaigned for principles not outcomes, the right to life, mutual respect, democratic principles … not a united Ireland or Britain." Michael has been a tireless fighter for human rights as well and works as an activist supporting the Organization for Security and Co-Operation in Europe (OCSE). His decades-long history for secular and civil rights include fighting against Ireland's blasphemy laws, fighting for women's reproductive health rights, the defunding of public religious education, gay rights, and the right to self-determination with regard to assisted suicide for the terminally ill.

He approaches atheism with a similar mindset. His life is guided by where the "evidence leads" him. The principle here is truth. If new evidence were to be revealed, he would change his direction accordingly.

Michael grew up culturally Roman Catholic in a 1960s Ireland where the church had great influence on the state. Most of the primary schools were Catholic and the nuns still wielded their leather straps. But Michael's parents were not religious—his home was a liberal "island of sanity." He had the benefit of a close family and the heartbreak of losing his nineteen-year-old brother in a motorcycle accident. At that point "trivial things" ceased to worry him and he began to take a look at the "meta issues."

He read a book on how to be successful that outlined a series of exercises, the bottom line of which, for Michael, was that success meant to achieve happiness. And upon further thought, he concluded that happiness involved having both good relationships and a sense of purpose. Activism combined both.

Today, the church has less control over the country. This year, they led the world in popular vote to legalized same-sex marriage.

Michael references the World Value Survey in arguing that society is moving from "religious to rational values." As president of Atheist Ireland, he is pleased to be at least a small part of a "multigenerational" movement in that direction: a direction from "survival to self-expression values, a direction where science replaces religion," a direction of "wide human change."

....

HOLLAND

MARIEKE HEIKENS

MARIEKE TAKES HER atheism for granted. Many of our questions baffled her because it is difficult for her to imagine being anything else. In an attempt to understand what drives religious devotion, she read *Why God Won't Go Away* by Andrew Newberg, a nonfiction work that presents the neurobiology of belief. Learning about the brain science behind the belief in a god helped her make sense of the lure of religion.

Marieke had a religious, churchgoing grandfather who, although married, was homosexual. She sees his religiosity as being fear-based, perhaps a fear of going hell for his sexual orientation. Her mother attended Catholic school but Marieke told us "church beat religion out of her." Her father was Protestant, but neither parent raised their children with religion.

Marieke has a master's degree in humanitarian assistance, as does her husband. Before working at Oxfam, she worked for the International Rescue Committee in Afghanistan and in the Democratic Republic of the Congo. At home in Holland, Marieke has no close friends who attend church, but in Congo, she was surrounded by faith-based humanitarian agencies, which gave Marieke an opportunity to be planted among aid workers who were both funded by a religious organization and motivated, at least in part, by faith. She even found herself at times wishing she was religious because she said she was "jealous of the consolation" that comes from prayer.

Marieke concludes that there is no difference in the quality of the work done in the field between those serving due to religious reasons and those who are atheists. But as you will see, our man from Greece disagrees.

....

GREECE

GEORGE PETROPOULOS

GEORGE PETROPOULOS IS Greek, and he is hardcore when it comes to atheism. He even has a tattoo on his ankle to prove it. After all," George proudly states, "atheism is a Greek word meaning absence of belief." He was baptized Greek Orthodox but was raised in what he considers a secular family—one that is "religious in the European tradition," as he describes it. George's background is in international affairs, conflict resolution, and international security. At the time of the interview, he was working on safety and security projects in war-torn Afghanistan as Program Director for the Norwegian Refugee Council in Kabul, Afghanistan. Before that, he had spent eight years as country director in both Uganda and Pakistan for Action Against Hunger. At thirty-five, he is forward-thinking, quick-minded, and laser-focused on making this world a better and safer place.

George likes his humanitarianism secular. He feels aid workers with religious motives are not pure in their agenda and therefore are a different breed of humanitarian entirely. He distinguishes between assistance and charity, feeling that helping others should be the "human imperative" of every human being. "It was Jesus who said 'love thy neighbor'….just man up and be a good person. You live once and there is no paradise or hell," George says.

Though there are still secularist issues to be concerned about—even as the Greek military still recites evening prayers—George is an optimist about his fellow man and the future of atheism. He feels that social media is giving atheism a home and believes that we will see a large increase in nonbelievers in the coming years. And he is confident about the Hellenistic Atheistic Union's actions in challenging the lack of separation of church and state in court.

UNITED STATES
MIKE I.

SEPTEMBER 11 MADE Mike I.* feel "useless." At the time, he was working for a large bank and all of a sudden, the world of finance became insignificant to him. He had been living in New York City since he was eleven years old, and he wanted to help his fellow Americans.

Realizing the importance of national security, he decided to enlist in the United States Army Reserve and quickly became commissioned as an officer. He went through basic training at the age of forty in Ft. Jackson, South Carolina, and qualified as a civil affairs specialist in the "diplomatic branch" of the army.

While serving in the Army, Mike tried to focus as much as possible on the relevant national security issues at hand. With his background in engineering and management, he was often bothered by the inefficiency of the military, like the frequency of ceremonies and all the resources wasted on them. To make matters worse, chaplains were required to say prayers to the captive audience in front of them.

And Mike was an atheist. Having been born in Odessa, Ukraine, then part of the Soviet Union, no one in his family was religious (though his documents list him as "Jewish"). Religion was irrelevant to Mike and to his circle in the Soviet Union.

Yet Mike's written complaints about prayers went unanswered, so he eventually felt it was his duty to speak up and let everyone in his unit know that the prayers were disrespectful to nonreligious service members, causing vocal backlash from the old guard and the religious right. At the same time, it stirred up a conversation about the incompatibility of age-old traditions and the modern Army value of nondiscrimination based on religion (or lack thereof). Though some humanists advocate for the addition of humanist chaplains, Mike believes the entire Chaplain Corps is no longer relevant to the modern military and refers to it as "an ugly mess, no matter how you look at it."

In December 2012, he was deployed for nine months to Djibouti where Mike first became involved in humanitarian assistance. His task force joined with African partners in order "to maintain a stable environment...an Africa that is stable." Some of the projects his unit accomplished included digging wells, building schools, distributing bed netting, and establishing medical clinics for the local populations. His task force also participated in "the exchange of best practices with the local nation armed forces."

Mike returned to America in September 2013, relieved that "the 9/11 decade was over." Now he is speaking out against the religious right in the United States, Russia and Ukraine, where bitter battles over religious education in public schools are still being waged. Though many issues still keep him up at night, at least he no longer feels useless.

*Name withheld by request

....

INTERNATIONAL

DALE MCGOWAN

IN 2006, DALE MCGOWAN resigned from his university teaching position in Minnesota, moved with his wife and children to Georgia, and began his second career as philanthropist and author.

He wanted to identify the "gaps in the atheist humanist community" and figure out how to address them. He discovered that religious communities participated in charitable giving by a magnitude of two to three times more than atheists. He believed that this was not because atheists did not want to help people but because they did not have the needed systems in place for charitable giving. In 2010, he launched Foundation Beyond Belief.

He has also written two parenting books, *Parenting Beyond Belief* and *Raising Freethinkers*, both of which are secular parenting guides for raising moral children without belief in god composed of advice from experts and from Dale's own background. Dale grew up attending a Protestant church every Sunday, but there were no prayers said at meals or before bed for the three sons of this working-class American family. His parents encouraged Dale and his brothers to "find the wonder and chase curiosity," and to think out-of-the-box. A self-declared atheist since the age of sixteen, Dale and his wife have also raised their children in a secular home.

Dale's father died unexpectedly at the age of forty-five from a cerebral aneurism when Dale was thirteen years old, at which point he developed a "profound interest in mortality" that he feels brings "life into focus." When Dale reached the age of his father's death, his focus shifted from conducting a college orchestra and teaching music theory and history to a leap into philanthropy. He and his three employees developed Foundation Beyond Belief while working for minimum wage until last year, when a large donation allowed for his dream to jump several levels. Now Foundation Beyond Belief has five categories of charitable giving: education, poverty and health, human rights, the natural world, and "Challenge the Gap," a category featuring progressive, non-proselytizing religious charities.

Foundation Beyond Belief makes it possible for nonbelievers in the United States to donate on an ongoing basis and as a direct expression of their worldview. At this time, the foundation has ninety-five teams of volunteers around the United States and one international team. Dale is reaching his goal to "energize the under-engaged portion of the philanthropic world:" the nontheists, the unaffiliated but humanistic people, and others who never had a platform for organized giving.

Dale is always searching for the next "gap" and his "hope is to continue creating secular alternatives to human needs formerly fulfilled by religion."

....

ICELAND

HOPE KNUTSSON

HOPE KNUTSSON WAS a radical left-wing demonstrator on the streets of New York City protesting the Vietnam War, nuclear power plants, and the inequitable American healthcare system in the hopeful generation of the 1960s in the United States. In those days, you could get a cheap flight to Europe on Iceland Air which included a stopover in Iceland for twenty-four hours. Every hippie who wanted to see Europe flew with them. Some even smoked pot in the aisles of the plane, and when they landed, they took the popular Golden Circle tour of volcanoes, waterfalls, and geysers before moving on to their destination the next day. Hope took one of these flights and fell in love with Iceland's beautiful "sane Nordic society" which had no military and where tax money was used to help its citizens—she called it "paradise on earth." She moved there, "married a Viking," and is now seventy-one.

Hope's life is defined by helping others. She has worked as a psychiatric occupational therapist in hospitals, aftercare centers, and group homes. She has headed a support group for the rights of the mentally ill at a mental health association, organized public lectures, and regularly writes a newspaper column in Reykjavik addressing mental health issues. She has participated in setting up a school of occupational therapy. As a pioneering American immigrant and humanist in a nominally Lutheran country, she founded and ran an English-speaking foreigners association and a multicultural council to assist and advocate for immigrants from many countries. She wrote a newspaper column about culture shock and intercultural marriages.

But perhaps what Hope is most proud of is her current work. In Iceland, the majority of thirteen-year-olds get confirmed in the Lutheran state church. When her children reached that age, they refused to be confirmed because they were not Christian. Hope reached out to the Norwegian Humanist Association to help her develop an alternative. She then founded civil confirmation, a secular coming-of-age ceremony, in Iceland and became one of

Godless GRACE ⋮ 63

the founders and current president of Siðmennt (Sidmennt), the Icelandic Ethical Humanist Association.

Sidmennt offers a three-month course for teens, taught mostly by philosophers, to prepare them for their secular confirmation, covering topics like ethics, critical thinking, human rights, human relations, equal rights, relations between the sexes, skepticism, getting along with parents, protecting the environment, being a teen in a consumer society, and what it means to be an adult and take responsibility for one's opinions and behavior. Their diploma reads, "Broadminded, tolerant, responsible person of great integrity."

What began as a small grassroots movement in 1990 has exploded." It took many years of lobbying Parliament, but in 2013, secular humanists finally won the battle for equal legal and funding status. Secular weddings are now also legal in Iceland, creating a higher demand for secular celebrants.

This change in law lags behind Iceland's reality where fewer than 50 percent of the people are religious. Iceland also ranks ninth out of the top ten nonreligious countries in the world in a recent international survey,[12] and 86 percent of Icelanders accept evolution over creationism.[13]

Hope is grateful she was raised in a secular home. She asserts that atheism is a necessary first step on the road to humanism. She quotes Thomas Paine: "My country is the world, my religion is to do good."

Her parents named her Hope because she was born with a cleft palate and wouldn't be able to form certain consonants like T, S, or D until she could have the necessary surgeries and speech therapy. Perhaps her parents had more in mind than that for a daughter who needed hope to weather her younger years and for the hope she would come to offer others for her entire lifetime.

CANADA

ROSS MUTTON

AT EIGHTY-FOUR years old, Ross Mutton is still helping people to stop drinking—but not through Alcoholics Anonymous. A former hairdresser and a self-described former "heavy drinker," Ross feels qualified to help the working-class population of Calgary, Alberta, lead better and more sober lives. To this end, at age seventy-three, he returned to school and obtained his PhD. His first book, *Rational Addiction*, is about to be released.

Ross grew up in a small rural town in Ontario, Canada, the son of a dentist whom he describes as an "intellectual" who played golf while his mother brought him and his two sisters to church. His sisters remained religious but Ross did not, and his mother thought he had "lost his compass." He relocated to Calgary, a town defined by the oil industry and populated by people who moved there from Texas—it was a heavy drinking town where he formed his addiction.

But Ross discovered Jack Trimpey's California-based alcohol addiction recovery program "Rational Recovery." The program made sense to him and worked. Ross believes that Albert Ellis's Rational Emotive Behavioral Therapy is the most effective way to control an addiction and finds the seventh step in the Alcoholics Anonymous program that requires participants to invoke a "higher power" excludes alcoholics who can't believe in a supernatural power. He also found it antithetical to finding one's own innate power to "stop habits."

After his own recovery, he is now helping alcoholics in prison with Rational Recovery. Rational Recovery is a paradigm shift that has not yet caught on. Ross attributes this to the balm of community that Alcoholics Anonymous provides. Ross's dedication to "reason" led him to a recovery program based on "intentionality instead of magical thinking." His desire to help others has led him to spend his later years spreading the word about an alternative to twelve-step programs that not only helps nonbelievers but people of faith as well. Perhaps as the atheist community continues to grow, so will this behavior modification technique be adopted, helping all people to feel more empowered in their road to recovery—not only from alcohol, but from all addictions.

....

EGYPT
HASSAN KAMAL ELDEN
HASSAN ABDELHAMEED

HASSAN KAMAL ELDEN Hassan Abdelhameed is relatively new to atheism. He's from what he calls an "ordinary" religious Muslim family, but his passion for philosophy started him on the road to questioning. By age twenty-seven, he stopped believing in god completely. Socrates's "denial of Greek gods" was his entry portal to open-mindedness. From there, he read "Bacon, Paine, Spinoza," he listed—before laughingly adding Richard Dawkins.

Believing that "philosophy is everything," Hassan sees nonbelief as the cornerstone of humanitarianism. Disenchanted with Egyptian law, he stopped practicing as an attorney in 2009 and began working to improve the lives of his people as a program officer for the El Sadat Association for Social Development and Welfare. In 2012, after the revolution that took down President Hosni Mubarak's government, he served as parliamentary assistant to the Chairman of the Human Rights Committee of the People's Assembly until it was unfortunately "cancelled" in September of that year.

Hassan believes secularism is a prerequisite for democracy, even though what he describes as "political Islam" remains the governing tool of his country. And that the Internet and social media contribute to what he calls "e-democracy," which is a tool that can exponentially expedite the elimination of "7,000 years of taboos" in regard to Arab "sensitivity" to secularism. Social media has "spelled death for time and place," said Hassan, referencing that speed at which social media can enable social transformation.

To that end, he has created a website and an electronic magazine, *SecularEgypt.com*, in order to contribute to the secularization movement. "It is not safe to say you are an atheist, but it is okay to work for secularization," he explained. His magazine quotes the liberal Saudi writer Ibrahim Albleahy who cries out for Arab societies' "need to evolve into liberal societies by acknowledging their backwardness and modeling themselves on what Western nations have gone through when they emerged from the church-led backwardness of the Middle Ages."

Even though recent events in Egypt suggest that he may not see secularization in his own lifetime, Hassan has not lost any of his passion in the fight for secularization and democracy.

．．．．．．．．．

BRAZIL
ELIAS VIEIRA ARAUJO, JR.

IT WAS EASIER by far for Elias Vieira Araujo Jr. to come out as a gay man than it was to come out as an atheist. Growing up in a very religious community, one of four children, Eli was born and raised in the Brazilian state of Minas Gerais in a town of five thousand people. His mother is Catholic, his father is Protestant, one of his sisters remains Catholic, and his other two sisters became Spiritists, becoming part of a growing Spiritism movement in Brazil (best known for the influential, now deceased, medium Chico Xavier).

Religion is a complicated situation in Brazil. Democracy was reestablished after a twenty-one-year-long military dictatorship, and in 1988, separation of church and state was once again reinserted into the constitution. But like in the United States, religion is influential in politics. In 2007, three years before running for office, the current President of Brazil, Dilma Rousseff said, "I balance myself on this issue" when asked by the press about belief in god. But fear of the loss of potential votes resulted in Ms. Rousseff 's rebranding of herself as a believer. She emphasized her "supposed Catholicism," as Eli describes it, and she started attending masses in honor of the "Holy Mary of Aparecida." Her popularity surged, ultimately winning her the presidency in 2010 when she became Brazil's first female president.

Eli himself was the first president of the Secular Humanist League of Brazil (*Liga Humanista Secular do Brasil*, LiHS), founded in 2010. He now serves as the Director of International Relations at LiHS while simultaneously working toward his PhD in genetics at Cambridge. At the age of twenty-eight, he is well on his way to making a difference in this world on several fronts. When Eli's mother discovered he was an atheist, he reassured her that he "accepted the values [she] taught" him, and he does. Although he is an empathic man, Eli does not believe "the bedrock of morality" should lie in empathy. He sees empathy as potentially dangerous because of the tendency to empathize only with people we agree with. "The state of the art in reason and philosophical ethics relies on reason," he explained.

Eli is most proud of his organization's rapid response to the 2013 Kiss nightclub fire in Santa Maria in southern Brazil that killed two-hundred people. Through their strong internet presence, Eli and LiHS were able to raise and deliver money for medication and supplies for the survivors. In 2010, LiHS organized a one-hundred-city campaign against stoning to help save Sakineh Mohammadi Ashtiani and others from execution in Iran. In 2011, their organization protested against rape, sexual harassment, and misogyny in Brazil. By supporting a bill introduced by their congressman, honorary LiHS member Jean Wyllys, they work for complete decriminalization of prostitution so that sex workers are not exploited by pimps.

In the LGBTQ arena, Brazil makes it difficult for a transsexual to change his or her name. LIHS is working toward making that an easier process.

The issue of lynching has also become a serious problem in Brazil. The Secular Humanist League is demanding the cessation of the practice.

While currently studying at Cambridge University, Eli is also translating, from English into Portuguese, the works of Susan Haack, who he admiringly calls "a hell of a thinker."

While growing up in his small farm community with no atheists, Eli read Bertrand Russell's autobiography and thought "[Russell] lived a wonderful life." You can feel the excitement in Eli's voice as he contemplates the continuation of his own wonderful life.

MEXICO

GERARDO ROMERO QUIJADA

GERARDO ROMERO QUIJADA had too much time on his hands one evening at his IT job. While surfing the web, he stumbled upon the site for British Conservative Catholics (BCC), where they listed helping parents stop their children from masturbating was one of their missions and that they had a facility to save these "genital stimulators from Satan." Gerardo "thought it had to be a joke," but it wasn't. The BCC also linked to atheism sites as examples of the work of Satan. In curiosity, Gerardo clicked on these sites, read what they had to say, thought about it, and eventually "de-converted from Catholicism into atheism." Ten years later, he became the main organizer of Mexico's first National Atheist Conference in 2010. He currently hosts "Masa Critics," a weekly two-hour radio talk show in Mexico City promoting skepticism—Unintended consequences for the BCC!

Thirty-nine-year-old Gerardo had grown up as a devout Catholic. He went to church on Sundays, prayed daily, and even went to receive blessings before every school exam. He told us he was a "very good Catholic, better than most." In 2000, after receiving his undergraduate degree in computer science, he did a graduate student exchange program in Ottawa, Canada. One requirement was a philosophy course, and ethics was the only course available. This was Gerardo's earliest introduction to the idea that a person could be "good apart from religion." He followed that line of thinking "down the rabbit hole" into agnosticism, a word he "had never heard of before," and rested there awhile. After his discovery of the BCC website, he read and re-read George H. Smith's book *Atheism, The Case Against God.* Realizing that "compartmentalization led to cognitive dissonance," Gerardo resolved into nonbelief.

Although Catholicism is on a steep decline in Mexico, it is the evangelicals, the Mormons, and the Muslims who are absorbing the ex-Catholics. This worries Gerardo because he believes that "the Catholics are lazy, but the Evangelicals are activists" and can potentially change the consciousness of the Mexican people to a "righteous intolerant one."

Gerardo is eager to help people and "to make this world a better place." A few years ago, when Gerardo's organization, Ateos y *Librepensadores Mexicanos* (translates as the Mexican Atheists and Freethinkers, AyLM) was more active, they were able to do such things as supply laptops to schools that needed them. They also supplied free legal aid to people who couldn't afford to pay for legal advice, because they had members who were also lawyers.

But unfortunately, lately AyLM has stalled. There are no funds and few members. The economic hardship and violence of the last fifty years has made many Mexicans self-protective. The lack of trust has led to lack of giving—warm, kind people have had to stifle their generous natures.

When ex-clergyman Dan Barker (interviewed in the next chapter) visited Mexico City in 2013 to "apologize for teaching nonsense to your country," Gerardo accompanied him to the Basilica at Our Lady of Guadalupe, a pilgrimage site in Mexico City, where Dan witnessed children walking on their knees to honor the Virgin Mary. Dan was gripped by a sudden urge to stop the children, and Gerardo had to restrain him from intervening. The experience was a bittersweet moment for Gerardo, not unlike his journey of trying to make his country "a better place."

....

·····.···

I want to understand the world from your point of view.
I want to know what you know in the way you know it.
I want to understand the meaning of your experience,
to walk in your shoes, to feel things as you feel them,
to explain things as you explain them.
Will you become my teacher and help me understand?

–ETHNOGRAPHER JAMES P. SPRADLEY

....

CHAPTER 2

GODLESS GRACE – FROM CLERGY TO ATHEIST LEADER

INTERVIEWS WITH FORMER CLERGY

SPECIAL FOCUS: CLERGY COMING OUT ATHEIST

In 2011, through a donation from the Richard Dawkins Foundation for Reason and Science, the Freedom from Religion Foundation formed a support group called The Clergy Project to help former clergy who have become atheists come out of the closet and speak openly about their transformation from ministers, priests, or other clergy member to advocates for nonbelief. Since The Clergy Project's inception, more than 450 former clergy in the United States and abroad have joined this support group.

These clergy-members-turned-atheist are taking leadership roles, writing books, and maintaining blogs and other social media outlets to let their fellow atheists know about their activities and thoughts. They use their notoriety to help others less fortunate in the nonfaith as well as in the faith community.

Men and women who were formerly "of the cloth" serve as a vital link and are at times quiet emissaries to those religious leaders who remain in the closet but who have also lost their religious faith. They show through their actions that although leaving organized religious faith behind is difficult, it is monumental in shaping their worldview and activism going forward. Many of the former clergy, who were trained in how to better bring the "good news" of faith to their flocks, now use that same energy and training for a different purpose entirely.

The former clergy hope to not only liberate the thinking of their religious constituents but also to show them that, if current and former representatives of the higher echelons of their faith can be morally upstanding and socially vital without a god, so can they. They demonstrate that religious spirituality and supernatural dogma provide too small a way to think about who and how community should be defined.

They are also beacons for their fellow nonbelieving clergy who are tied to their communities who fear rejection or who worry about their family's social and financial wellbeing. They demonstrate how The Clergy Project serves as a waystation and social community for closeted clergy who now have a place to seek emotional support from their nonbelieving peers.

On a side note, it is understood that some clergy members may choose to keep their doubt to themselves even as they preach and perform religious rituals. They may serve as the only safe harbor for members of their community who need a shoulder to cry on or to share a confidence. This is the case in places where their tabernacle may also serve as more than a place for religious worship. It may serve as a community space and meeting hall, food bank, a homeless or women's shelter, a space to teach literacy, or a place to hold Alcoholics Anonymous or Narcotics Anonymous meetings. To disengage entirely can be a very painful decision for those who know that their absence may leave gaps of support and service in their communities.

For the following section, we interviewed some former clergy members. They all now dedicate their lives to preaching the good news of living an evidenced-based and moral life without the need for a personal god. They are also helping other current and former clergy come to peace with their own questioning, skepticism, and nonbelief. The former clergy discuss their nonbelief and view of faith, their values, and their aspirations. They also talk about the loss of careers and community and difficult decisions that accompany the coming-out as nonbelievers and how to deal with friends and family members who remain deeply religious.

These interviews highlight the growing number of former

clergy who are taking the "good without a god" mantle to their local communities and around the globe.

MADISON, WISCONSIN

DAN BARKER

WHAT DIFFERENCE DOES NONBELIEF MAKE IN YOUR LIFE?
We spoke with Dan Barker via Skype and discussed his history as a preacher, his second career as a leader in the freethought movement, and his many books, public appearances, and work as co-President of the Freedom from Religion Foundation.

Barker reflected on his own journey in the activist atheist movement: "Early in my preacher days, most of my reading was within Christianity and Christian philosophy, but towards the end of my believing, when I hungered for meaning, I began to read Robert Ingersoll and Bertrand Russell."

As he grew in the movement, his ideas about nonbelief also matured. He explained, "Atheism is like having a large debt cancelled but humanism puts the money in the bank. When you become an atheist and activist you're like the person who pulls weeds from a planter. Atheism is pulling the weeds. It brings you to zero, cleans your slate, and is like a double-negative, like nonfiction. It opens your eyes to truly helping yourself and others."

But humanism has become central to Dan's identity because it serves as a locus and practical way of seeing others: "When there are no threats, I think our instincts are to be both altruistic and sympathetic.... It's only when things are bad that we become physically and emotionally violent towards one another. I believe that the headlines do not represent our daily lives. The human things we do out of kindness just don't make the headlines."

When asked why this way of thinking was important, Dan responded, "There is no meaning or purpose to life and that's good! Purpose is almost secondary. The fact that there is no purpose of life doesn't mean there isn't a purpose in life. Purpose and meaning come from trying to solve problems."

He personifies this purposeful way of living when confronting problems that arise in his own life. "I try to do better next time because I'm a glass half-full person. I am and always will be an optimist, I can learn and improve internally and not place blame on the system or others. That's the freedom of not thinking in terms of sin or sinners."

How Do You View The Question Of Faith? Dan often writes about his former days as a regular churchgoer, a preacher, a Christian songwriter, and a Protestant missionary. Dan powerfully recounted what it felt like to evolve away from his religious faith: "I didn't lose my faith, I got rid of it. Although religious faith is comforting to many it isn't a tool to gain real knowledge. [It's] a shield of ignorance. What sharpens your mind is reason and living an evidenced-based life."

Dan is a member of the Lenape Indian tribe from along the Delaware River. The tribe was Christianized in the 1830s. He told us his people characterize this indoctrination as both a form of imperialism and as "the religion of the invaders." "It's the same everywhere, from Mexico to the Apache, even for the medieval Jews of Europe. So many were forced to convert to avoid reprisal and then intergenerationally forgot their old ways, and we all forgot that we were just pretending," he explained.

Although early life in the Barker household was religious, one of Dan's two brothers and both of his parents eventually became atheists. As an adult, Dan continues to have friends and acquaintances that cover the spectrum of religious and spiritual belief, but many of his friends are also now atheists. Of his religious friends he noted, "We all know each other well and they certainly know my activism and really, we get along fine." Dan's daughter is an active churchgoer and his grandchild, following in Dan's earlier footsteps, is a Christian musician. But Dan humanistically related to us, "When we're together we always talk about the things that unite us as a family rather than what may separate us."

On Compassion And Death: What Nonbelief Values Are Most Important To You? Dan Barker's social and legal contributions in securing and strengthening secular civil rights through the Freedom from Religion Foundation have set the standard for many humanist activists. According to Dan, he values his nonbelief because it's a clear and direct connection to reason and a release from emotional captivity. "Atheists for the most part are inner-directed," he shared during our conversation. "Believers submit but nonbelievers think for themselves," he added.

When we chatted about personal responsibility, Dan's focus was again on rationality and what science has to tell us about the inner workings of our evolution and brain chemistry.

"Our morality comes from being mere mortals. We all can be compassionate and have passion for this world without faith, as it's sort of our original setting biologically to be empathetic. We don't need religion to tell us how not to harm one another.

I think the best way to be moral is to create the least amount of harm to our environment and also to try to live our individual and collective lives causing the least amount of harm to one another. I call that the "harm principle" and it's discussed in more detail in my forthcoming book."

Dan jokingly told us that he's not afraid of death, but he just doesn't want to be there when it happens. "Most atheists feel that same calmness in that there was a universe before we were born and that we'll return to it after we're gone. Frankly, if life was eternal it would cheapen the overall experience of our personal histories and experiences."

WHAT ARE YOUR HUMANIST ACTIVITIES AND ASPIRATIONS?

Dan Barker noted that his organization has had numerous legal victories regarding the separation of church and state, and he's most proud of the debates where he's moderated or challenged clergy on First Amendment issues. "I'm also proud of my books and the impact they've had. If I can spread the love of learning to help people grow and change I feel like I've been successful," he said.

Dan's self-acknowledged high water mark includes first creating and now financially supporting The Clergy Project through FFRF: "So far we have almost six-hundred clergy join The Clergy Project and seek counseling. About a quarter of them are still preaching from the pulpit. "We're now giving many of those who came out nonbelievers hardship grants to readjust since most participants lose their jobs and standing within their communities. But this is a positive sign that secularism is growing. What started in the United States is now an international movement."

NEW YORK, NEW YORK

DAVID MADISON

WHAT DIFFERENCE DOES NONBELIEF MAKE IN YOUR LIFE? New Yorker David Madison, former-minister-turned-atheist-leader and member of The Clergy Project, also sees what's substantially good in others. First and foremost, the idea of "coming out" meant several things for David. It was not just about coming out atheist. It was first about coming out gay after years of marriage and church leadership. It was later in life that coming out as a nonbeliever and activist became as important to him.

"For me, coming out as an atheist was a transition based on reading and knowledge for my own personal growth," said David at the Manhattan hotel where we spoke. He said that Timothy Ferris's book *Coming of Age in the Milky Way* and Carl Sagan's original *Cosmos* series each had an impact on his identity and his ideas about nature.

His own book, *10 Tough Problems with Christian Thought and Belief: A Minister-Turned-Atheist Shows Why You Should Ditch the Faith*, delves further into his conclusion that the theology of Christianity falls short of the humanist message it tries to present: "All you have to do is look at these anti-gay laws in Uganda and see the face of radicalized Christianity. You really have to marshal your arguments to say God and faith are good...These are life and death struggles... It is the struggle against the apocalyptic nature of evangelical faith. Look at those who are climate change deniers: almost all of them are evangelicals who approach science from a religious perspective."

He declared that, "there is an arrogance and imperialism in religious faith. It's a mindset which accepts evil as part of God's grace—acceptance that evil is part of God's bigger plan, which I think is a shallow answer. In part that is why I left the clergy. After all, what kind of god are you tolerating when you say the Holocaust and all kinds of hate like it is part of God's plan?"

David believes that both atheism and humanism are more in harmony with the environment and with living well with others, and it's through his understanding of science that his atheist activism and humanism emerge: "We have these mammalian brains, we have good brains which work towards compassion and make art and literature and wonderful things for humans to enjoy but we also can be 'monsters.' So the answer can't be found in theology to make us better, it has to come through secular laws and helping one another humanistically."

HOW DO YOU VIEW THE QUESTION OF FAITH? David Madison had a mother who was a devout conservative Methodist and a father who was a teacher and physician. But in their case, "conservative" did not mean fundamentalist; both accepted evolution as the way God had engineered life on earth. Growing up in rural Indiana in the 1940s and 1950s meant church every Sunday. It was seen as an important social obligation, which the whole family took very seriously.

While David's mother did not go to college, she was a serious bibliophile, especially when it came to religious studies. She purchased the twelve-volume *Interpreter's Bible*, a product of liberal Protestant scholarship that was usually owned and read only by ministers and preachers. David told us that he "had religious faith all through college, but [his family] believed that the Bible didn't have to be taken literally. Questioning was encouraged—everything but the existence of God."

He continued, "I was always interested and challenged by the epistemology of faith. You know, how do we know God? Do we get closer to him through prayer, meditation, visions, experience? None of these ways of knowing are verifiable and it began to eat away at me."

In the end it was this questioning and lack of verifiability which broke David free of his religious faith: "It was easy to let go. I began to doubt when I began seminary school and by the time I finished my PhD in biblical studies, I became an atheist... Even a simple thing, like how far up is heaven, is problematic. Two thousand years ago, heaven was in the clouds, then science showed us what was in the clouds and heaven became more ethereal, not so much a physical place but a metaphysical dimension. But theologians have been forced to turn too much to metaphor. Sure I cannot prove to you that there is no god but I can discuss the probabilities of their existence—as Richard Dawkins has so famously pointed out. And then when we do that, we don't limit the discussion to the gods you may or may not believe in but all the gods."

David is especially proud of his humanist activism, his long relationship with his husband—also named David and also a committed atheist—and his daughter who is also candid about her nonbelief. "I'm glad to say that my two grandchildren are getting a secular upbringing as well," he remarked.

ON COMPASSION AND DEATH: WHAT NONBELIEF VALUES ARE MOST IMPORTANT TO YOU? In contrast to Dan Barker, David takes an opposing view of his mortality: "I think everyone fears death and I certainly fear it. Not the dying part so much but perhaps not being able to say goodbye properly, or to live long enough to see the next big thing."

He remembers when Christopher Hitchens said that the worst part about it all is "knowing the party will go on without you," and when Carl Sagan said he'll miss knowing how history turns out. "That's exactly how I feel about leaving the stage," David said. However, while he's among the living, David remains directed towards helping the causes he's most passionate about, namely gay rights and atheist activism. He is now retired, but for more than thirty years in his business career, he helped people find jobs, using humanism as a guide:

"Being a humanist has naturally shaped my work. I've spent a lifetime helping thousands of people, directly and indirectly, get the best possible jobs so that they have higher self-worth and the ability to feed and shelter their families... Certainly being decent to one another is how society succeeds. Murder and robbery cause problems and laws grew out of these negative human experiences. Our current secular laws are based on nonreligious, commonsense values that are the most healthy for our society."

And he disagrees with the claim that atheists have no moral compass: "I have always rejected the conservative claims that atheists have no moral compass. In fact, religion has played a major role in derailing morality. For example, anti-Semitism is very much a Christian created phenomenon. Just read the Gospel of John and some of the statements of St. Paul. There you'll find the roots of anti-Semitism. And Martin Luther was virulently anti-Semitic. Why would anyone name a denomination after him? Christianity offers just as many examples of moral blindness as moral wisdom."

David quoted Richard Dawkins—"Those of us who are alive are the lucky ones"—when it comes to both mortality and morality." It all comes down to compassion for others, empathy, and asking how can I correct a social problem in the least religious way possible. Certainly don't pray for me, as that's a cop-out. Keep an action orientation and help those less fortunate locally if that works for you," David concluded.

What Are Your Humanist Activities And Aspirations?

David Madison's focus for many years was helping people find adequate employment. "After leaving the clergy, the road was bumpy for a while, but I ended up in a helping role, and the awe I felt at transforming lives was inspiring. It was good to put the theology baggage behind me and perform work that really helped people better themselves. So I'm proud of my legacy done in the name of my secular work."

"And using humanist ideas of reason also helped me because those tools for finding rational truth allow me to help others focus on accessible and right-fit jobs based on their education, skills and experience. When people wind up in the right job their lives can change forever."

Ultimately, David is proud of his daughter's work and hopes she will continue his freethought legacy: "She is a professional genealogist, and does it so well because she is a fanatical researcher, which means she is a gifted historian. She's been digitizing and posting letters between my parents—her grandparents—who wrote to each other every day when they were separated during World War II. That's thousands of letters and she researches the historical background reflected in the letters. Being interested and supportive of her work is part of my legacy as well."

.....,.....

DE RIDDER, LOUISIANA
JERRY DEWITT

WHAT DIFFERENCE DOES NONBELIEF MAKE IN YOUR LIFE?
Ex-Pentecostal pastor Jerry DeWitt is known for his effervescent speaking style, his passion, and his transformational story from Bible Belt preacher, to Clergy Project member, to atheist activist and national speaker. We spoke to Jerry while he was driving home from work. He pulled over (ironically into a church parking lot) to speak with us via phone about his history and ideas regarding nonbelief, how the movement has shaped him, and how he is shaping the movement.

"As you know, I got the Holy Spirit when I was sixteen-or seventeen-years-old and was profoundly moved by being born again," he told us. However, this induction into evangelical ministry wasn't entirely suppressive, Jerry explained.

"Even when I was preaching and being preached to the constant drip of reason filled me with wonder. I had this voice of reason, mostly through my friend Dwaine who was a big influence, helping me to ask questions, which is a very scientific thing to do. When I eventually came out as a nonbeliever it was like that scene in the *Phantom of the Opera*. I had just been limiting myself to Southern gospel and although it moved me emotionally to feel the Holy Ghost, I was also deeply confused."

"But my faith tradition was, and is to those who do believe, somewhat scientific, although it is based on spirituality. We were brought up to have an evidenced-based Christianity, we had to look for signs of God and signs that you were a child of God to prove we were worthy. It's when I came to my humanism that I finally lost that religious surety and dogma."

He saw that other religions and forms of spirituality have the same form of confirmation bias that his own faith required. "If you accept that the Ouija board works it will work, same like religion, even if there is no real evidence except for the feeling it gives you."

And with this loss of spiritual religious faith came an awakening in Jerry towards a new way of viewing himself and helping the world.

"When I lost that surety I was left in a completely secular venue, none of which was inspired by the Holy Ghost, and what I took from faith made me secular. My skill set evolved to where instead of me preaching and taking action for religious faith, I now channel this into secular causes. I now speak a secular message brought through my training as a religious preacher."

As a humanist activist, he feels that he can appreciate the being moral and being alive even more.

"I accept that people are good because our social networks allow us to be good. We are biologically driven to pursue pleasure and avoid pain, but this is the biological basis for existence as we can only feed our own stomachs and pass on our own genes. By being good we ensure a healthy world."

"Guilt and shame are corrupting and confusing, which is why religion for some of its beauty and meaning is so painful. From the humanist point of view, we are empowered to equally appreciate the gift and complexity of life. In fact, seeing reality and life without divine purpose doesn't leave a world without meaning. We give life its meaning and we see the value of living secularly. Certainly this is what I conclude gives my life meaning."

Jerry ended on a very positive note, expressing the importance of understanding nature: "From a humanist perspective, I cannot overexaggerate the positive effects of understanding nature. Treating internal and external nature religiously is sort of selfish, but humanism allows me to tolerate my own feelings, no longer influenced by an invisible good or evil being. I'm left with the same feelings that my ancestors felt but I deal with them differently—not as though my feelings are corrupting and outside of nature. But understanding that they are part of nature and that we are all part of the same nature."

How Do You View The Question Of Faith? Unlike for Dan Barker, for Jerry DeWitt, there was no feeling of religious invasion when it came to his growing faith and participation in the Pentecostal movement and religious world. He grew up in the Deep South with a grandmother matriarch who was deeply religious. Pentecostalism was natural and felt like a good fit; it was a duty to carry the tradition forward at home and in the community. In fact when it came to other areas of knowledge Jerry amusingly noted, "There was never any talk of Darwin. The closest we got to any discussion on evolution in my school was a brief section on pollination in my biology class."

As he writes in his recently published autobiography, *Hope After Faith: An Ex-Pastors Journey from Belief to Atheism* and as he shared in our interview, "[The Pentecostal] life exists in its own world, its own ecosystem with clear boundaries which certainly demark and will often demonize other sects within Protestantism along with other faiths in general."

But for Jerry, it was with what faith didn't provide him that he was so frustrated. It didn't lead to a profound truth or to brotherhood. As he recounted to us, "Faith, as I was taught, separated me from myself and therefore it separated me from others. It didn't erase those invisible lines." It was only when he left preaching and embraced humanism that he began to feel the human connection he longed for. "It was the acceptance of nature that erased those lines for me: those lines which removed barriers to my own self-knowledge and from truly learning and understanding others," he said.

Jerry remains close to friends from his former religious community. Many of them stood by his side as he lost his preaching job, the security of his home, his social status, and very nearly his wife. But the one person who stood by him the most was his son, who is also an atheist. "Honestly, if my son became religious, which I know will never happen, I'd feel that it would totally restrict his human potential. Even so, I'd love him no matter what he chose," Jerry proclaimed.

ON COMPASSION AND DEATH: WHAT NONBELIEF VALUES ARE MOST IMPORTANT TO YOU? Jerry's values of nonbelief are framed in the notions of transcendence. "I suspect my secular activism is based on a religious motivation, that is, fulfilling a personal vision for worldwide revival but this time through nontheistic belief and through a secular message of love, understanding, and hope, which I see as making me less naïve and more effective in the real world...Once you see people being people you gain a greater appreciation of life as a whole as there is no invisible evil source controlling our actions."

"Nonbelief has created for me a sense of oneness with the world that I always wanted and never fully had through religious doctrines of faith. Before becoming an atheist I could not love my neighbor because I could not fully love myself.

"I have always lived by the Golden Rule which is to treat people as I wish to be treated and do the least harm. At the same time I also truly value self-expression, which is something in organized religion that can be frowned upon."

As for what comes after this life, Jerry approaches death matter-of-factly. "I'm not worried about what happens," he said. However Jerry did add rather whimsically, "I'm not really afraid of death, I'm just afraid of dying."

What Are Your Humanist Activities And Aspirations?

Just as David Madison decided his legacy is tied to his children, so too does Jerry DeWitt initially focus his contributions and legacy on a future for his family.

"I've accomplished a great deal since coming as out an atheist a few years ago, but I give much credit to my son who helped me survive the turmoil that it caused in my family life."

"I think I accomplished a significant amount just in terms of adding to the demographic puzzle of the Deep South with my coming out, my public appearances, and my book. I've shown that you can come from a very religiously conservative part of the United States and not only survive but thrive as a nonbeliever. I think I've helped express that there is a great deal of complexity to clergy who resign from the pulpit for atheism. I am just as human and even more caring but I don't serve a religious theology any longer."

Jerry also sees his personal advocacy transforming as he moves deeper into the nonbelief movement: "I think secular humanism really needs to build a bridge to those who would consider themselves open and cultural Christians. In my ideal world when one identifies as a Christian it should be synonymous with just being a good, moral and ethical person. I can contribute to making this happen because I've served on both teams. Christianity may never go away but it could just evolve into a metaphor and then we'll have helped move us to oneness."

But a legacy outside of what he leaves his son and immediate family is equally important. He told us, "If I could teach people to have self-confidence which derives from self-appreciation and self-love, I will have accomplished a lot. So much harm comes from self-loathing that it's so unbalanced and anti-humanist."

And for Jerry, being good without God is straightfoward: "Being good without God is, in part, looking at your reflection and liking what you see. We can't anthropomorphize our deities any longer, and we have to grow up."

"We can win the war of ideas by having everyone love their neighbor as we love ourselves."

·····

·····■·····

We should be teaching our children the scientific method and the reasons for a Bill of Rights. With it comes a certain decency, humility and community spirit.

–DR. CARL SAGAN

CHAPTER 3

Godless Grace – Rise Of The "None" Activists

The Rise Of Young Secular Humanist Activists

The number of people under thirty who claim no faith or do not identify with any organized religion is growing internationally. Since young people are often the most socially and politically active, it should come as little surprise to see this liberation of thought and action to change society and help those who perhaps cannot help themselves.

As in other social movements, youth culture has played a large role in the Arab Spring uprisings that started in 2010 and the attempts to install secular government in tyrant-led regimes. The Occupy Movement, which began in New York, became an international youth phenomenon, dedicated to trying to change society though changing social priorities, economics, and the idea that we must take care of those who are less financially well-off.

Humanist student groups across the United States and internationally have sprung up to help others. According to the Secular Student Alliance, on hundreds of college campuses and in high schools, secular student groups organize blood drives, travel, and perform rebuilding efforts after tornados or hurricanes, and eagerly partner with faith-based organizations, NGOs, and government agencies to assist those less fortunate. They aid the sick, provide care for the poor and elderly, give legal advice or medical help, and teach and help communities build infrastructure after some natural or manmade disasters.

For instance, members of the William S. Boyd School of Law Secular Legal Society provide free tax services to the poor regardless if they are religious or not.[14] At the University of Alabama, nonbelieving students raised funds for the Leukemia and Lymphoma Society rather humorously through their "Send an Atheist to Church" program.[15] At the end of the fundraiser, the students would go to the particular house of worship marked on the cup with the highest contributions for a Sunday service. In perhaps a more serious but equally inventive vein, you've already been introduced to the Pathfinders Project, a part of Foundation Beyond Borders that has sent four students on a year-long service journey around the globe to support clean water, education, and sustainability projects in countries across Asia, Africa, and Latin America.

It should be acknowledged that there are numerous religious groups who are allied with international government interventions and NGOs in order to send young people as resources to help devastated communities globally. However, religious missions of help typically bring with them missionary work, and sometimes provide support only when those being helped accept Bibles, prayer or Bible classes, or even communion in order to receive the convenience of clean water, shelter, education or health care. Religious organizations sometimes may even forgo the help of secular activists to propel their beliefs.

For example, in 2013, right before Thanksgiving, a group of nonbelieving students and other freethinking activists in the Kansas City area attempted to support a local mission by delivering meals to the poor and elderly. But they were turned away from assisting.[16] The reason for the rebuff? The local mission was delivering these meals in the name of their religion and not, as the nonbelievers had assumed, in the name of a shared humanity.[17] Earlier that year, in Spartanburg, South Carolina, another group of young and seasoned activists were barred from serving meals in a local soup kitchen although they had no intention of revealing to the clientele their nonbelief. And again, the reason for rejection was the group's denial of a supreme being. In both cases the activist humanist groups only wanted to help those in need. Their purpose was not to create conflict nor was it their goal to gain publicity by being turned away.

But in the twenty-first century, a growing number of students are providing support for communities harmed by poverty or other forms of deprivation without the need to recognize any particular faith as a motivation to do good works. In the United States, where approximately 15 percent of the population claims to be nonbelieving and religiously unaffiliated, the number of eighteen to twenty-nine-year-olds who define themselves to be atheist or agnostic stands at 22 percent.[18]

That double-digit number equates to almost a quarter of all Millennials and Generation Xers who are in high school, post-secondary education, or graduate and professional schools. They are all potentially activists who might perform humanitarian work at home and around the globe. And on campuses and high schools they are supported by humanist chaplaincies, clubs, and service learning groups which enhance and validate their sense of community as well as their efforts to help others through charity work and fundraising.

At least three secular agencies have helped to provide a constructive outlet where for students can serve others. The Secular Student Alliance, Foundation Beyond Belief, and the Camp Quest movement each work directly with students and have a leadership structure where those who were formerly activists can now help younger generations find their secular voice and socially connect like-minded children and young adults.

The interviewees in this section are students and the next generation of leaders in the nonfaith movement who are currently dedicating their lives to secularism and atheist civil rights. Many of them felt isolated among their peers during their high school years because of their nonbelief, but began to take leadership positions in the nontheist movement once they went off to college or entered the workforce, where they met more diverse and like-minded people. As with the clergy profiled in Chapter 2, each interviewee is actively working in the name of humanism to support the freethinker movement and also working in some field to help others.

NEW HAVEN, CONNECTICUT

ALEX DIBRANCO

WHAT DIFFERENCE DOES NONBELIEF MAKE IN YOUR LIFE? In speaking with several activists in their teens to early thirties, we found graduate student Alex DiBranco to be a fine representative of the emerging humanist leader demographic because of her social justice work and advocacy for women's and LGBTQ rights.

Because of Alex's generation and place of birth in the northeast United States, she found nonbelief rather early in life and didn't really think much about its implications. "I wasn't really influenced by anyone, to tell the truth, but I always liked the philosophy of Nietzsche and Albert Camus," she said.

Although her transformation was less dramatic than Dan Barker's or David Madison's, it wasn't any less formative. "My nonbelief matters and it is important because we only have one life to make better," she told us. "It's important not only to be a nonbeliever, but it is equally important that we live in and maintain a society where people can be atheists."

To Alex, choice, freethought, knowledge, and activism are all deeply held values. But it is through her nonbelief and openness to build bridges with both faith-based and nonfaith organizations that she finds her work to be most productive.

She, like many in her demographic, is not a so-called "angry atheist," and she seeks to work with any person or group who share similar goals regarding justice and helping the abused. As Alex sees it, "People are basically good or are born a blank slate. We are not essentially evil and I don't believe as a humanist that people are predisposed to harming others versus feeling good by helping others."

As to how her nonbelief impacts her world view she explained, "I'm still trying to figure it out, but I do think we all have to be concerned with our own personal happiness and that of others. The trick is harmonizing this to make this a better world."

Alex also shared how she copes with hardships in her own life: "I try not to get angry but when I do, I go dancing to work out my personal problems. I don't think I'm an optimist or pessimist—I'm more of a realist. This life is all there is, no grand plan, and it isn't fair. Accept it for what it is and don't blame someone. Just figure out your way and don't get agitated, because there isn't a divine plan. It will help you remain centered and balanced."

HOW DO YOU VIEW THE QUESTION OF FAITH? Alex DiBranco describes her childhood as "technically Catholic," but religious faith was always at arm's length. "Sure I was baptized but I never had a communion ceremony and when we went to church it was once a year for Christmas, which also attracts many nonreligious people."

Because she never felt a schism with faith, her road to nonbelief was more smoothly paved: "By the time I was in high school, I was a self-described agnostic and when I was an undergraduate at Dartmouth, I embraced "atheist" as a more accurate term.

"Because I grew up in the Northeast, we learned about evolution in school and studied existentialism in English class. But I can understand why people need or want faith and progressive religious systems which work to help feed the poor and help those in need, especially women. I am aligned with that on a policy and activist level."

For all of her social activism, Alex remains open to having dear and deep friendships with people who are believers. "Most of my friends are on different places on the religious spectrum. But there is real variety and I don't want to close myself to any people or the potential to experience others," she said.

A friend of Alex's who plans a ministerial career recently decided to attend divinity school at Yale. Alex's perspective is, "I respect his religious perspective since it is aligned with my more secular view of healing the world."

ON COMPASSION AND DEATH: WHAT NONBELIEF VALUES ARE MOST IMPORTANT TO YOU? For Alex, what's most significant and valuable about nonbelief is the reality it brings to the world, which in turn motivates her to be an activist. "We need to change now and not in some afterlife. This is our one time to make a stand, to help as many people as possible." As an activist involved with feminist causes, Alex suggests that religion in some ways influenced the woman's movement, but acknowledges that organized faith has also been misused against women. "Nontheists and humanists were of major significance to the women's rights movement, which I consider a significant illustration of the power of humanism for activism," she said.

The rationality of nonbelief brought Alex to activism at a very early age. She told us that she became very involved in social action as an undergraduate. She helped promote the awareness of sexual violence and joined nationally affiliated campus groups such as Amnesty International. Through her journalism, she wrote about perspectives of atheist students on her campus as well as student gender and sexuality issues, sexual assault, and feminist issues.

Alex added, "I also worked for Change.org where I ran their women's and immigration rights and human trafficking blogs as well as worked on issues related to undocumented student deportation. Later, at Political Research Associates, I supported investigative journalism related to a host of issues like ex-gay therapy, right-wing religious movements and religious liberty, and access to healthcare and contraception."

On her humanist values, she focuses on four areas that she says inform her activism, advocacy and writing: "I'd say they are essentially not to harm anyone, to try to alleviate the suffering of others, have respect for people's human and civil rights as well as their bodily autonomy and work to understand our cultural differences."

WHAT ARE YOUR HUMANIST ACTIVITIES AND ASPIRATIONS?
Although perhaps too young to decide on her legacy, Alex DiBranco is certainly building an expansive resume regarding her humanist accomplishments. "Foremost it's important that people identify me as an atheist, because people don't understand what atheism is really about," she said. For Alex, it's really all about bridge-building between herself, her friends. and the communities she serves. "There's a lot that can be done between secularism and interfaith groups when they work together. Also I had a Catholic friend who had learned that atheists were bad people, but because she knew me she understood things differently."

Alex also told us what she was most proud of: "My work on behalf of women's reproductive rights, support of the LGBT community, fighting poverty and homelessness and generally people's rights regarding their sexual choices are each important to me and vital for helping those in need. I never want people to be ashamed of their sexual choices based on conservative morality. We have to challenge the US Christian right because they're attempting to remove civil rights at home and supporting the anti-gay laws in Uganda."

The tenets of humanism inform Alex's values and motivate her to work with others. "Secular humanism is my belief system and is at the heart of my humanitarian work."

....

Humans

STEVENS PORT, WISCONSIN

AMANDA METSKAS

WHAT DIFFERENCE DOES NONBELIEF MAKE IN YOUR LIFE?
Amanda Metskas was a youth activist. Now in her early thirties, she serves as the executive director of Camp Quest, a network of summer camps aimed at children from freethinking families. "As a very young person I didn't even know there was a nonfaith community," she began as we discussed her early life growing up in Wisconsin. "Although my dad was a quiet nonbeliever, when I was in high school, I read letters to the editor of our local paper by a local atheist about the problems with religious doctrines, including the similarities between Mithras and Jesus."

As an activist, she also doesn't mind the label of "atheist" although she understands that it can have a negative connotation for some. "I'm happy to use any title for my nonbelief, but the word 'atheist' matters because people are familiar with the term. It's just a conclusion that there is no god. Without such belief we are then free and able to examine the evidence and contours of reality," she said.

But leading an evidenced-based life is important because she views it as foundational to taking action in the real world to educate and help others.

"There are those people who are good and will be good regardless of how deeply they hold their religious beliefs and of course there are those who can be real jerks, too." (Though, according to Amanda, it's the same with nonbelievers.)

While discussing how her humanism has shaped her view about people in general she says, "I think that people are basically good. That is, for the most part. We have evolved to be prosocial in order to live in groups and survive, and we're certainly not sinful the way religion defines sin. So much is environmental. When you set up a healthy environment, you get good behavior; set up toxic incentives and you get toxic behavior."

Essentially, Amanda accepts that this world and our lives are transient and that we have a duty to make this life better both for ourselves and others: "We create meaning and purpose from several sources but mostly from the social connections from being with other people. That's what motivates me as an activist—to leave the world a bit better. Having people who I can count on, like my partner August, and a support network helps me when I'm struggling with depression and anxiety. Being open about my struggles is a way to reduce stigma, and let other people know that they can achieve their goals even with mental health challenges. Going out and getting help is a sign of strength."

It's this focus on strength which motivates Amanda to help others find their network and support those in need. "It's all about paying it forward."

How Do You View The Question Of Faith? Amanda Metskas always had doubts and questions about organized religion. She told us that she "never really believed but my mom took me to religious events and Lutheran religious school. But I only did the community service without going to the classes. My dad was always a doubter and it created tension and was a source of conflict in my home growing up."

"I never could get my questions answered and although my church was very moderate with very middle-of-the-road views, faith was always outside my interest and willingness to let go of my doubt," she said. Ironically, it was Amanda's consultation with her minister, who had recommended many religious books to help her that ultimately closed the door on her faith. After a long discussion, he said, "You just have to take a leap of faith."

This non-answer settled the question of religious belief for Amanda: "From that point on I could never believe and it wasn't because the church didn't have good people in it. It was because the nature of religious faith requires you to accept concepts without evidence and I just lack that willingness to accept ideas without proof.

"In fact when I think back about my community's church I see it was actually pretty progressive. They were ordaining gay ministers, and doing really good charity work by sending food abroad to the hungry so it wasn't that the people weren't nice."

The idea of religious community service can serve as a deep source of conflict, especially for those who view religious faith and public service as diametrically opposed to true charitable support, but Amanda views the work of her early church years more humanistically. "They were doing the good work that I wanted to do, but in the name of religion, which is something I couldn't accept as my way of helping others," she explained.

Amanda was placed with her family as a small child through a Lutheran adoption agency, so her non-religious ways did create conflict at home. She recalled that her "mother did feel pressure to bring me up Lutheran because of the agency's expectation that children adopted through their services should accept and embody the Lutheran faith."

She does speak proudly of her work today: "Today my work for Camp Quest lets me blend my activist roots and willingness to help others, especially as my work with the campers is so rewarding, since—in fun ways—we teach critical thinking and how to use reason and questioning. Doubt is healthy, doubt ensures we question, doubt allows us to learn. Also, we have a very active leadership program which allows our counselors to grow and take leadership roles in secular agencies as well as at our camp sites around the nation."

While she is religiously faithless, Amanda's extended family includes Jehovah's Witnesses and she continues to have many friends from diverse religious traditions. "Those who respect what I do understand that this is how I choose to help the world and on that level, we can all recognize that we're all trying to have a good life with the skills, passions and interests we've developed."

In talking about her own future, Amanda said, "I don't have children of my own at this time, but if I did, I'd want them to be secular humanists. But if they chose to be religious I'd be really scared for them if they chose Scientology. Organized religion can provide a sense of community, so I'd be more open toward them if they wished to explore Buddhism or even reformed Judaism— anything that would first allow for values which include compassion and autonomy."

ON COMPASSION AND DEATH: WHAT NONBELIEF VALUES ARE MOST IMPORTANT TO YOU? For Amanda, acting in the interest of humanity is the most important value: "We need to be part of this world for each other and ourselves. Only we can make this planet the way we want it so we have to get out there and do something. It's a real call to action."

Amanda recalled for us her own journey to activism. "I was vaguely aware of the organizations connected to nonfaith as a teenager and I began to work for the Student Secular Alliance and other humanist and atheist groups all the way through graduate school," she told us. From an ethical point of view, Amanda tries to intellectually excite younger children and teens towards freethought. "It offers the opportunity to grow and explore using reason," she said.

"Although atheists sometimes get pigeonholed as militant, I like to share subtle freethought books like the ones written by Doug Adams and certainly Richard Dawkins's *The Magic of Reality* because each speaks to the awe and wonder of the natural world," she noted.

To be in this world, according to Amanda, means we have to take responsibility for one another. "I think reason is a form of compassion, and the definition of humanism is really reason and compassion in action," she explained. "Evolution favors survival and we've evolved empathy and trust to build safer communities. We can't and won't survive alone."

Regarding an afterlife, Amanda sums up her feelings about death philosophically: "Being dead is like not being born yet. It's not painful or scary, it is just non-existence." Of course, like her fellow humanitarians, it's the way her life may end which concerns her most. "I've been exposed to good and bad ways to die, and I certainly don't want to go alone or in pain. If I could plan then I would be surrounded by friends and family and have effective doses of pain management," she said.

"It's really sad to have such a finite amount of time on the planet. It motivates you to get out there and use your limited supply of days well," she added.

What Are Your Humanist Activities And Aspirations?
Amanda Metskas acknowledges that there are hundreds, possibly thousands of faith-based summer camps, but the Camp Quest camps are the only ones in the United States which offer a humanist and science curriculum taught by humanistic and scientific counselors. Amanda thinks that her legacy is in the experience of every camper who comes to a Camp Quest site over the summer: "Camp is about growing up, it's about gaining independence and blossoming. I love working with kids and counselors alike to grow them into reasonable, rational and humanistic adults."

And Camp Quest does not discriminate. Religious families are invited and do send their children to the camp as well. "Tolerance is part of humanism so we never reject anyone or their history, values or beliefs. When you come to Camp Quest you become part of our secular family," Amanda said.

The Camp Quest system is growing. In 2003, there were just two camps—one in Ohio and one in Tennessee—and they had fewer than fifty campers. Amanda wants to grow the camps into every state and internationally when possible, and she has. "Last summer, we had almost 900 campers in twenty sessions at fifteen camps in the United States. Now we have two international camps as well."

"And our system of oversight focuses as much on leadership development of staff as it does to make sure campers have an awesome time," Amanda said. "We begin to train our counselors from about the age of fifteen to develop teens emotionally, using secular humanism as a guide." As the counselors grow up they frequently take staff positions in Camp Quest. Even if they don't, both campers and counselors return yearly. "We build such a strong community that people come back year after year. That's a legacy I'm most proud to support," Amanda concluded.

....

COLUMBUS, OHIO
LYZ LIDDELL

WHAT DIFFERENCE DOES NONBELIEF MAKE IN YOUR LIFE?
While Lyz Liddell has always felt a detachment from organized
faith, there were many people who shaped her nonbelief growing
up. Her advocacy work within the Student Secular Alliance keeps
her connected to her roots and the future of the freethought
movement. "Now, I think back and can see why I believe the way
I approach nontheism is by creating the biggest tent possible. It
is from my earliest influences. As a global culture I think we're
leaving supernatural faith behind and eventually we'll have a
religion-free society," she told us.

Her worldview allows her to take personal responsibility for
her life. "What it comes down to is a worldview without a supernatural additive. Nonbelief allows you to claim agency over your
own life and enhance your autonomy. It allows one to build an
emotional capacity to see others as equals....Secular humanism
pushes compassion for oneself and others, it shows that we're all
so similar without needing theology to tolerate our individuality."

Self-reliance helps to keep Lyz moving forward in her work and
personal life. "Stuff happens. You just have to pick yourself up
and dust yourself off and sometimes laugh or cry. Heck, crying is
good. It's all part of being human," she said.

HOW DO YOU VIEW THE QUESTION OF FAITH? Faith for Lyz
Liddell meant attending church services with her family, but she
never felt quite at home. "I was baptized and confirmed and was
even part of a religious youth group. But when I got to college I
stopped pretending," she said. Although she neither felt oppressed
by faith nor had any negative experiences as a youth, she always
felt distant from the practices. "Now I love the rituals and if I go
to church, it's to participate in the 'showmanship' of rituals and
to be present for others and not because I'm forced to believe,"
she said.

Although Lyz was baptized and confirmed, her parents were not very religious. As she explained, "They were receptive to Catholicism but less to the dogma and more to the spirituality of the faith. If we needed the church for anything it was for the support network."

Towards the end of his life, her father did become more religious. "My dad re-found his faith prior to his death," she said. "But religious belief is all mythology. It's like trying to put a square peg in the round hole of evidence and reason."

For Lyz, religious belief can best be summed up as an unnecessary extra. "I'm not spiritual per se, but I do feel a sense of wonder and appreciation for the world and everything in it," she proclaimed.

Lyz continues to have good friends from childhood who are religious: "Being open to others is important. But also I'm glad that growing up in Illinois I had a solid foundation in rationality, science and good sex education classes—none of this abstinence-only dogma."

This rationalist perspective is why Lyz thinks the humanist movement is growing. "It's about personal liberation and being good to all people. It's sort of like the prisoner's dilemma, even if we're inherently selfish, our humanity pushes us to be good."

ON COMPASSION AND DEATH: WHAT NONBELIEF VALUES ARE MOST IMPORTANT TO YOU? Through the Student Secular Alliance, Lyz Liddell has been able to translate her interest in community building, atheist activism, and humanitarian work into profoundly moving projects with teens and college students across the country: "Since 2008, we've grown widely in high schools and college campuses nationally. I'm proud to say that our involved students do service projects everywhere, like work at food banks or raise funds for dozens of causes. We've really done an excellent job at getting students out to donate blood. Sometimes 200 or 300 students will volunteer their time or donate."

SSA also offers students a safe place to come out as atheists. "This is the twenty-first century and even today our nonbelieving students face harassment, even death threats from certain people and communities. This is very brutal and SSA is working to offer atheist students safe harbor, letting them know they are not alone and that there are loads of people just like them in our country."

She went on, "We're also looking at collaborating with the humanist campus chaplaincies growing on campuses like the one at Harvard. I'm also a big fan of the activism of Dale McGowan, especially as it relates to how he's activated students to help those in need and to support environmental service projects around the globe."

According to Lyz, all this student-focused humanitarian charity work, in the name of helping others rather than in the name of a deity, shows that we can indeed be good without a god.

WHAT ARE YOUR HUMANIST ACTIVITIES AND ASPIRATIONS?

"I think I'm growing the student secular movement and that for me is an important legacy," said Lyz Liddell. Before SSA, there were few places nonbelieving students could meet or conduct community service work. Lyz's direction and mentorship over the last six years has had a profound impact on teens and students wishing to make a difference in their world.

She noted, "It's not my job to tell people to be atheists but to catch those who already are, and provide them a safe landing place."

Lyz explained that, "We've gone from a scrappy little organization to one that has received national recognition, and the community knows there is some entity out there which will back and protect their secular cultural ideas and traditions. Our work is simply about empowerment.

"When you can't talk to your parent or pastor about being an atheist or even questioning faith, we offer camaraderie.

"I'm also most proud to serve as a role model while at the same time work for an organization that does such great humanitarian work with students, while also protecting the civil rights of freethinkers and secularists regardless of their age."

....

PART TWO

*That we do not learn very much from
the lessons of history is the most important
of all the lessons of history.*

−ALDOUS HUXLEY

CHAPTER 4

...·.....

Non-God Belief In History
Some Of The Major Players And Ideas

The idea that there isn't a god, or that theology as a form of philosophical and ontological relevance will cause rather than solve human problems, is not new. While only some of the atheist humanitarians in this book may be scholars of the Greeks, or know of Baruch, Spinoza, or David Hume, they all echo in their own words and actions their concerns about faith in our modern lives. Such a stretch across the ages may leave the reader to consider the idea that nonbelief is actually as ancient as religious belief itself.

This brief introduction to the history of nonbelief is not meant to be comprehensive. It is meant to provide the reader with a succinct historical view of major philosophers, statesmen, and others who helped to identify and ask the fundamental questions about the value of God belief, religion, spiritual faith and religious ritual.

Elements of humanism can be found within the writings of early Chinese Confucianism and as a path to enlightenment for Indian intellectuals from Siddhartha Gautama, and no discussion about the philosophical history of atheism would be complete without discussing, at least in passing, the work and ideas of the atomist philosophers Leucippus and Democritus,[19] who were both pre-Socratic thinkers who propounded the idea that the natural world could be examined and explained.

At the same time, Diagoras of Melos, a sophist poet and critic of Greek mythology, examined the arguments for the divine and concluded there was no evidence for gods.[20] Indeed, the first glimmer of rational hope and wonder about the natural world may have been drawn as a line in the ontological sand at or about the fifth century BCE by these three Greek men.

In the third century BCE, the freethinker and philosopher Epicurus held that the world was governed by natural forces and not managed through any divine spark.[21] And it was the Roman poet Lucretius who in the first century BCE proclaimed, using Epicurean ideas, that not only are we and the universe governed by nature rather than divine mandate but that it's through chance that any of it exists at all.

One famous Greco-Roman statesman—also a philosopher, lawyer, and perhaps skeptic—was Marcus Tullius Cicero. Cicero was known to speculate, write, and orate on all sides of an argument. In *On the Nature of the Gods and on Divination*, his most famous work related to the nature of the supernatural, he offers multiple proofs for and against Epicureanism and the divine.[22] He suggests that if the gods exist, they do not care about the fate of humans; he also assumes the atomist's perspective in saying that all things, including the gods, must first exist in nature.[23] However, it is never fully clear that Cicero takes any side in these philosophical debates, as he often just presents the "evidence" for all sides.

The Dark and Middle Ages, brought on by the powerful theocratic and aristocratic nation-states of Europe and the Middle East, certainly delayed many opportunities for scientific discovery. But centuries later, during the European Enlightenment, Western civilization saw the rise of a robust doubt/skepticism movement championed by scientists, inventors, philosophers, and educated political leaders.

Seventeenth-century philosopher Baruch Spinoza, a Dutch Jew, was a critic of the organized Hebraic religion. He did not believe that God created the universe, and he conjectured that the deity didn't even exist. In addition, he also doubted the immortality of the soul. For his ideas, he was excommunicated by the Jewish authorities of the time.[23] Several centuries later, when asked if he believed in a god, Albert Einstein, another atheist Jew, was quoted as saying he believed in "Spinoza's god,"[24] meaning that he took the natural mechanics of the universe to be the all-powerful entity humanity had been searching for throughout history.

Eighteenth-century philosopher and librarian David Hume was one of the first enlightened thinkers to postulate that religion had no reasonable bearing on morality or the ability of humans to think and act in positive ways.[25] As one of the first true Enlightenment skeptics and atheists, his works had a major impact on naturalists such as Charles Darwin, on philosophers such as Immanuel Kant, and on other scientists including the man known as "Darwin's Bulldog," Thomas H. Huxley. So while the scientific method and a healthy skepticism certainly are not new, we can glean from Hume's writings that skepticism regarding nonbelief predates both the Industrial and Information ages.

American scholars and statesmen such as Thomas Jefferson and James Madison, both theists, were concerned with the possible impact state-sanctioned religion could have on freedom and constitutional democracy. The Founding Fathers of the American Revolution, the Constitution, and the Declaration of Independence, each wrote extensively on the dangers of mixing politics and religion. Jefferson literally invented the phrase "a wall of separation between church and state" to describe his feelings towards liberty and religion. Madison is credited as the author of the First Amendment to the Constitution, crafted to free the federal government of any state-sponsored religion and to eschew any government favoritism towards any particular faith.

The Industrial Age saw the growth of what some call a modern renaissance period for science, technology, and an understanding of how the laws of nature operate and impact the planet and our universe. The expansion of public education and university systems across Europe and America led to a more educated citizenry that earned higher wages and spurred an influx of immigrants to the US. This created a groundswell of intellectual and social change.

The paradigm shifts caused by three particular scholars from Europe would forever change what we know, how we go about obtaining facts, and the intellectual and physical tools devised to gain such understanding. Charles Darwin, Sigmund Freud, and Albert Einstein each challenged conventional ideas about faith, scientific truth, learning, personal responsibility, morality, and the nature of the universe. Each has, helped us understand and interpret the cosmological, biological and social forces which impact our lives.

Darwin's *On the Origin of Species* changed how we view nature; Freud's work in psychoanalysis changed how we understand the psyche and how we operate internally; and Einstein's special theory of relativity was a breakthrough in understanding how the universe naturally operates. Through their insights, they have given humanity, and by extension each of us, ways to rationally understand our world without the need for a divine hand in the making, operation or future of our universe.

This lack of acceptance of a personal deity leads us to a humanistic point of view where the locus of power and control of our daily lives and destiny resides strictly in the hands of each of us to maintain. Humanism is essentially a philosophy of action which leads those who partake to freely inquire about themselves and the universe while also placing the responsibility and means to improve our individual and collective lives squarely in human hands.

For humanists, like atheist activists, this means that they have to think about others and also share a collective empathy. Humanism includes concern for the emotional and physical health and the living standards of fellow people, other species, and that of the earth. Secular humanists are pragmatic; they tend to look, based on situation and experience, for the most immediate and best course of action in support of those in need.

While both ancient and modern religious faiths may espouse elements of humanism, the essential difference between religious humanism and secular or cultural humanism is that religious humanism is and will always remain God-based. This is a critical difference since one's actions, identity, and reason for existing then include being motivated to help others in order to please a higher spiritual authority. In secular humanism, there is no spiritual catalyst to trigger either the interest or motivation to help others.

The modern world of atheist thought is alive and vibrant with the work of so many scientists, educators, organizers, philosophers and intellectuals. Truly we stand on the shoulders of giants. In the twentieth and twenty-first centuries, the world has given us Madalyn Murray O'Hair, Carl Sagan, Stephen Jay Gould, and the "Four Horsemen" of Atheism: Richard Dawkins, Daniel Dennett, Sam Harris, and the late Christopher Hitchens. We also have writers and academics such as PZ Myers and Jerry Coyne each blogging about nonbelief in its relation to a scientific world-view. In the entertainment field, we have James Randi and artists such as Penn and Teller, Ricky Gervais, Sarah Silverman, Bill Maher, and a host of actors and actresses who are nonbelievers.

In the twenty-first century, atheism is finally out of the closet and also a political force. International surveys estimate that slightly more than one billion people may be godless (although in some cases they also may have spiritual lives).[26] In the United States, upwards of forty-seven million Americans claim no faith, identify as agnostic, or identify as atheist.[27] In Europe, atheism is growing by leaps and bounds as people turn away from organized religion.

We also now have social media to connect people in ways that, in the past, would have taken years to accomplish. We now have means at our disposal to quickly create and build communities and movements where it would've taken decades before. Social media has allowed us to connect, share information, and befriend like-minded people from all walks of life around the globe. Because of the Internet, one's socioeconomic class, ability or disability, ethnicity, language, gender and sexual preference, age, education, and a host of other personal or group labels mean little to nothing.

Dozens of nonprofit and social groups for atheists can be found and accessed online. These and a host of other private and public groups are all working independently and at times together—to create a world where secular democracy, humanism, and atheism can socially and politically thrive alongside or even ahead of the institutions of organized faith.

This may be why the people in this book graciously allowed us to interview them. They know what we know: that unless and until we share our stories, nonbelief may continue to be defined by others—those who wish to harm or castigate us as individuals, as a community and as a political and social force.

As the humanist philosopher and author A. C. Grayling so aptly explains, "[H]umanism is not just about humans in the sense of believing that the only worthwhile topics of moral and ethical debate are human beings and their societies….[It's] about behaving like the best of civilized, thoughtful, responsible, considerate agents…You expect humanists to be humane in all things, including attitudes towards nature and non-human inhabitants.[28]

····•····

····•····

When comparing this with previous generations under 30…
Young people today are not only more religiously
unaffiliated than their elders; they are also more
religiously unaffiliated than previous generations of
young people ever have been as far back as we can tell.

–GREG SMITH, THE PEW RESEARCH CENTER

....

CHAPTER 5

DEMOGRAPHICS:
WHERE ARE THE ATHEISTS?
WHY STUDY THE TRENDS

Nonbelievers are a large and complex group. They attract the interest of social scientists, theologians, and all those interested in the nonfaith community. Knowing both the possible and potential numbers of adherents to atheism, secularism or humanism, as well as those working or contributing in some allied field, offers social scientists, demographers, governments, politicians, businesses, organizations, and marketers information to plan for the future, create movements, and develop programs that cater to the tastes, beliefs, perceptions, wants and desires of those living without religious belief. There is substantial data on the number of nonbelievers in the world today. In this chapter, we will define and describe where they tend to do their humanitarian work, and how these choices impact both services and communities on many levels.

Data exists which allows us—to a reasonable and sufficient degree—to approximate and also locate the number of atheists in the world and in any given nation. These numbers are based on survey data garnered from numerous private agencies, academic clusters, religious organizations, and government censuses.[29] New and independent research is being conducted yearly to gain insights into trends related to nonbelief by organizations like the Pew Center, WIN-Gallup, the Barna Group, Atheist Alliance International, the United Nations, and a host of governmental agencies and academic researchers. Even the Vatican has been collecting data and studying local and global changes in religiosity for decades through its Central Office for Church Statistics.[30]

As is the case with most social science research related to demography, not all data is constructed equally. But even if we accept that only a portion of the information is useful, more than enough exists for us to judge trends and make inferences about the value of the collected statistics. We can easily agree with E. O. Wilson who stated, "We are drowning in information, while starving for wisdom. The world henceforth will be run by synthesizers, people able to put together the right information at the right time, think critically about it, and make important choices wisely."[31]

While statistics do show trends in nontheist belief and ways of life, there usually is both variation and cohesion within communities of freethinkers. Therefore, generalized descriptions, while necessary to define any group in terms of basic characteristics, cannot be assumed to be fully shared universally by all those within a given population. This is as true for atheists as it is for theists, or specific ethnic communities or economic classes or groups broken down by education, profession, or other way of life.

As with all populations that grow and become cohesive, the expanding number of "Nones" (people who claim "None" when asked in a survey or census about their religious preference) continues to grow, they will change society as they build their political and social base.

THE BIG PICTURE—NONBELIEF IN RAW NUMBERS

According to the Pew Center, 84 percent of the world's population identifies as religious, while almost 16 percent of the unaffiliated population does not identify as religious.[32] Within this unaffiliated group of approximately one billion people, many view themselves as spiritual but choose not to attend formal religious services or come from traditions that do not offer organized faith and rituals like those practiced with the Abrahamic traditions. Additionally, a growing portion of the globally "unaffiliated" also considers themselves "nonbelievers," or people who disassociate with organized faith entirely.

The 2012 Win/Gallup International Global Index of Religiosity and Atheism ranks nonbelief worldwide.[33] This organization, which surveyed more than fifty countries (covering more than 73 percent of the global population) found that eight of the top eleven nations with significant atheist populations are in Europe while three are in Asia. These include the Czech Republic, France, Germany, the Netherlands, Austria, Iceland, Australia and

figure 1: TOP TWENTY NATIONS: RELIGIOSITY BY NATION		
SURVEYED NATIONS CLAIMING TO BE LESS RELIGIOUS	SURVEYED NATIONS WHOSE RESPONDENTS ARE "CONVINCED ATHEISTS"	SURVEYED NATIONS CLAIMING TO BE MORE RELIGIOUS & LESS ATHEISTIC
China	China	Vietnam
Japan	Japan	Afghanistan
Czech Rep.	Czech Rep.	Ghana
Turkey	France	Malaysia
Sweden	S. Korea	Iraq
Vietnam	Germany	Azerbaijan
Australia	Netherlands	Tunisia
France	Austria	Georgia
Hong Kong	Iceland	Nigeria
Austria	Australia	Fiji
Netherlands	Ireland	Brazil
Azerbaijan	Canada	Macedonia
Canada	Spain	Romania
Ireland	Switzerland	Lithuania
Switzerland	Hong Kong	Turkey
Germany	Sweden	Uzbekistan
Spain	Belgium	Lebanon
S. Korea	Italy	Kenya
Finland	Argentina	Ecuador
Russia	Russia	Pakistan

© ORENSTEIN AND BLAIKIE

Ireland, South Korea, China and Japan. In some cases, depending on the nation, more than 70 percent of those responding claimed no religious affiliation or were self-described atheists.

Excluding the right-hand column of Figure 1 (on the previous page), whose respondents are from faith-based nations, the surveyed populations in the first and second columns show distinct national population trends related to nonbelievers. The first column reports on nations whose respondents claim to be less religious and the second column offers insight into the nations whose populations confirm their atheism. These are not agnostics, unaffiliated, or spiritualists outside of organized faith but a ranking of whole nations whose citizens self-identify as nonbelievers. Based on this data, this makes a total population of 834 million people living without organized religion. This total does not include all the other nations of the world and their nonbelieving citizens, including the United States, alone would add another 65 million people to the tally of unbelievers.

Conversely, data from that same study indicates that the ten nations with the least atheistic populations are in Africa, the area in and around the Middle East, Central and South America, and finally Eastern Europe. It should come as no surprise that formerly colonized nations within Africa and the Americas would remain religious since the religious beliefs and traditions brought by European settlers, along with the current number of missions—evangelical or otherwise—are often synonymous with the social welfare and aid being offered to indigenous peoples—some of whom have to rely on religious organizations as their only option for food, shelter or education. Within the Middle East, the strict purview of Islam and sharia law makes thinking blasphemous thoughts—never mind coming out as an atheist—very difficult. Five of the seven nations where apostasy is, under law, punishable by death are Middle Eastern nations.

In Eastern Europe, the fall of the Soviet Union released a huge amount of pent-up religious energy, as faith and belief could not be openly expressed during the time of Communism and the Cold War.[34] This in turn has kept the freethought movement from receiving much exposure and notoriety as Russians declare their faith or spiritualism openly. While in other European nations that are more secular and less hostile to freethinkers, the number of skeptics and nonbelievers continues to rise.

Since 2005, the nations whose populations appear to be turning to both nonfaith and secularism in great numbers span all continents and national boundaries. These countries include Vietnam (-23 percent), Ireland (-22 percent), Switzerland (-21 percent), France (-21 percent), South Africa (-19 percent), Iceland (-17 percent), Ecuador (-15 percent), the United States (-13 percent), Canada (-12 percent), and Austria (-10 percent). According to Win-Gallup data, the entire planet's global religiosity on average has shrunk by 9 percent since 2005.[35]

We may be able to attribute this shift to many causes, but access to social media and the Internet has had a significant impact on spreading ideas about humanism, secularism, and atheism. Use of electronic and social media is also helping people form social spaces (both real and virtual) where freethinkers can mingle, share ideas or just be in community. In one study conducted by Cornell University professor Allen B. Downey, his research suggests that access to the Internet led to significant decreases in religious affiliation from the late 1980s through 2010. The data notes that the Internet lead to an almost 20 percent increase in un-affiliation while other potential variables, such as college graduation, could only account for about a 5 percent decrease in religious affiliation.[36]

Regionally, the greatest number of nonbelievers are in North Asia, with 72 percent of the population either being self-described atheists or non-religious. However, this high number in Asia may be skewed if people are forced to claim nonbelief because of political oppression from regimes such as North Korea and China.

In Western Europe, 36 percent of the adult population chooses to live without religious faith. In North America (including Canada) about 33 percent of the population claims to live without a personal or communal god. The region where atheist numbers are the lowest are in the Middle Eastern countries considered political "flashpoints" by the United Nations and several global affairs think tanks. These include Pakistan, Iraq, Afghanistan, Bangladesh and Palestine; within these geographic and political boundaries, as few as 2 percent of the population describe themselves as non-believers. However, we can surmise that these numbers may be low because of the political and social pressure to either practice faith or be ostracized (or worse) by clan, the community at large, or the government.

These data discovery tools include census research, demographic profiles based on a host of achieved and ascribed demographics and finally individual or group interviews, which tend to shed a more intimate light on how and what people are doing and thinking to inform their lives and to help others less fortunate. Each of these methodologies brings to light different types of information with different levels of data clarity and complexity. So while none of the methods are fully descriptive, they do stand as the best, and at times the only, way to investigate the social trends, belief and actions of religiously faithless humanitarians and their communities.

WHERE DO ATHEISTS DO THEIR PUBLIC SERVICE WORK?

Atheists are socially organized and perform humanitarian works on every continent and in most nations. The United States has by far the largest number of recognized secular groups who support their members through community-building programs, political advocacy, or relief funding. These include, but are not limited to the Foundation Beyond Belief, Skeptics and Humanists Aid and Relief Efforts (SHARE), and Atheists Helping Homeless.

In addition to the nontheist groups listed above, we find the American Red Cross to be one of the leading secular nonprofit service agencies doing good work around the globe. The American Civil Liberties Union, the SEED Foundation, Goodwill Industries, Americares, Planned Parenthood Federation of America, the National Center for Science Education, the Human Rights Campaign, the Nature Conservancy, and the Union of Concerned Scientists are all chartered as secular social services, community services, and environmental nonprofit agencies as well.

In every Western nation and in countries across the globe, even in those states which barely tolerate secularism, strictly secular humanitarian organizations are helping the sick, educating the illiterate, and serving as intermediaries between clan members and the ruling local or state authorities. So we have the work of others in the Atheist Alliance International, the British Humanist Association, International Humanist and Ethical Union (IHEU). Because of their longevity, the Gora family (profiled earlier) is an important example—through the Atheist Centre in India, the Gora family has performed humanitarian work since 1940. Other agencies include the Tanzanian Children's Fund and various groups in India and Pakistan working locally in tribal regions to provide a formal education or healthcare to those without access to schools, the Internet, or hospitals.

Internationally, there are dozens of globally-based secular institutions where one can easily volunteer or support in other ways. In addition to UNICEF, we find Doctors without Borders, the United Nations Children's Fund, Amnesty International, Engineers without Borders, IPAS, Oxfam International, MADRE, ActionAid International, International Relief Teams, and Rotary/Rotary International—just a few of the organizations where humanitarians of all kinds fund efforts and volunteer to serve.

Hyper-local or micro-capped humanist groups exist to serve an immediate purpose and then disband, or offer their volunteers and donors to other groups until the service is no longer needed. So we have secular groups forming around human-made and environmental disasters or groups which help communities lift themselves out of poverty. These organizations include KIVA, which provides microloans to economically disadvantaged people so they can start small businesses; DonorsChoose, which allows people to provide school supplies to needy public schools; and PlanUSA, an international relief agency whose mission is to mitigate both short and long-term crises in more than fifty countries.

RECENT GLOBAL SURVEYS— THEIR IMPACT AND IMPORTANCE

In 2012, Atheist Alliance International began to collect self-reported data through their Atheist Census website to track and count atheists from around the globe. To date, more than 260,000 individuals from more than 200 nations have self-reported.37 The brief survey requests that the responder to elect which specific nontheist title they prefer. Choices include "atheist, agnostic, bright, humanist, rationalist." The survey also requests their birth religion, education level, age, gender, and nationality.

The overwhelming majority of respondents in all nations describe themselves as atheist. In addition, most respondents came to nonbelief from some sect of Christianity. Most of the responders hold at least an associate's degree, but, many have a bachelor's degree or higher. More than two-thirds of the nontheists answering the survey are male and the majority of responders are thirty or older.

With its relevance and up-to-date analysis of respondent answers, the survey offers strong insight into select atheist demographics. But drawing deeper conclusions may be misleading. The overall sample size of the survey and the mechanism itself may be limiting to the wider nonbelief community. For instance, in many places around the globe it is still difficult to locate a computer and access the Internet.

Additionally, nonbelief is a private matter for many individuals who may consciously choose not to participate in the survey. By its methodology, the data may be more reflective of a certain income, educational level, the ability to access the Internet, and the amount of social freedom responders have to safely answer the survey's questions.

Conclusions

There are large numbers of atheists who are active in their communities who self-report their nonbelief without fear of reprisals. However, there are other groups of nonbelievers who, based on their location, may not have access to technology or may not be freely able to share their nonbelief. This may skew census and demographic information and other data, but even if these variables were removed, the data that has been collected gives a clear picture of where the majority of nonbelievers live around the globe. Data collected from several unbiased and authoritative sources, including The Pew

Center, Barna Group, and WIN/Gallup amongst others, show that religious faith in many regions of the world is receding.

There are many secularists supporting social causes, political and healthcare initiatives, education and the environment. They may act individually or work through different types of organizations. Secular humanists have a great variety of choices and options in terms of giving both time and money to help others. These groups include, but certainly are not limited to, global nonprofit secular aid organizations, international healthcare agencies, social justice and environmental groups, education foundations and teaching communities, science foundations, microlending and micro-service organizations, legal defense agencies, cultural organizations, and humanist, atheist and freethinker organizations and associations.

There are also countless nationally organized and regionally located secular groups, and thousands of individuals in most geographic areas who help feed the poor, help out in underfunded schools, work for preservation of the environment, build houses for the homeless or rebuild whole communities after disaster strikes. Individual humanists do give money and more importantly they donate their time to support numerous charities and causes for the sake of making the world safer, richer and kinder.

………

·····•····

·····•····

Knowing there is a world that will outlive you, there are people
whose wellbeing depends on how you live your life,
affects the way you live your life, whether or not you directly
experience those effects. You want to be the kind of person who
has the larger view, who takes other people's interests into
account, who's dedicated to the principles that you can
justify, like justice, knowledge, truth, beauty and morality."

–STEVEN PINKER, COGNITIVE SCIENTIST

CHAPTER 6

·········

WHO ARE THE NEW ATHEISTS?

INTRODUCTION

A theists come from all walks of life. Atheism knows no ethnic, economic, political, gender, social or demographic class. The New Atheist community is boundless. It includes its modern internationally known spokespeople, but it also includes its lay leadership and all of the people who attend secular meetings or gather to share their ideas concerning nonbelief. This chapter explores both the personality and reasoning of people who choose atheism to inform their perceptions and lives.

The position that there is no supreme being comes from both a skeptical tradition as well as one founded in rationality and scientific thinking. For instance, there's a strong correlation between people who are atheists and people who work in the physical sciences. In a 2009 Pew survey, the organization found that 33 percent of American scientists believe in a supreme being, while in the general public that number is 83 percent with another 12 percent believing in a higher power other than the Judeo-Christian God.[38] Being a scientist, however, doesn't automatically make you an atheist. For example, Dr. Francis Collins, the head of the Human Genome project and the National Institutes of Health, is a practicing evangelical Christian who appears to have harmonized his scientific work with his faith and belief in a personal God.

Atheists can be liberal or politically conservative, rich or poor, formally or self-educated and socially progressive or not very open to progressive thinking. The Barna Group's research on religious belief and socially liberal and conservative populations in the United States found that 11 percent of liberals identify as atheists, while just 2 percent of conservatives do.[39] Seventy percent of the conservatives interviewed in that study said their faith was increasingly important to them as they aged, whereas only 38 percent of liberals felt this way. Finally, as a political consequence of faith and nonfaith, liberals are less likely to place moral authority in the Bible or see it as a source of truth, and have less need to consult God, the Bible, or any religion when making political and social choices.

Coming to terms with one's atheism and freethought in the course of performing humanitarian work can bring with it a host of positives and also some negatives. On the positive side, atheists who work for the public good feel like they are making the world a better and safer place by putting their efforts and energies into the very humanity which they hope to support and inspire. However, choosing to be an atheist can be a negative in areas and nations which do not support freethought. The International Humanist and Ethical Union (IHEU) often reports incidents of social and legal discrimination, emotional intimidation, and even violence towards atheists, humanists, and secularists by many governments, making nonbelief dangerous in many places around the world.[40]

NONBELIEF: THE STATISTICS
Rise Of "The Nones" As An American Demographic

In the last decade, those who have been counted in survey data and who claim no faith have been labeled "Nones" by statisticians, the media, and those in the nonfaith movement. This group is defined as simply having no faith or affiliation with any house of worship.

In 2012, the Pew Center conducted a survey on American religiosity. They found that since 2007, the percent of those claiming affiliation with religious groups has fallen by 5 percent from 78 to 73 percent while at the same time, the percentage of those claiming atheism, agnosticism or no faith in particular has risen to over 4 percent, from roughly 16 to 20 percent.[41]

Since 2007, the trend in nonbelief appears to have risen amongst most age groups. However, the groups with the lowest overall religiosity are baby boomers and the generations that fol-

low which include Gen Xer's and Millennials, essentially anyone
born after 1963.

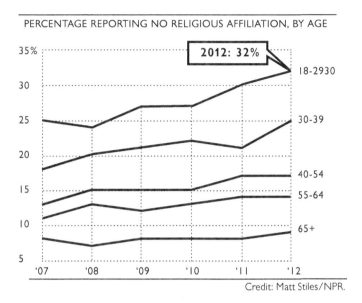

PERCENTAGE REPORTING NO RELIGIOUS AFFILIATION, BY AGE

2012: 32%

18-2930

30-39

40-54

55-64

65+

According to the chart, which is based on Pew Center research,
there has been an increase of 3 percent in nonbelief for those
born between 1946 and 1980, and an increase of 4 percent for
those born after 1981. The survey also indicated that those born
after 1991, who are known as the "younger millennials," begin
their nonbelief journey as a demographic at a full 34 percent,
meaning that more than one in three people in this age group
do not accept a personal god. In total, the research found that 20
percent, or one in five American adults, either do not have a religious
affiliation or do not practice any faith.

RECENT STATISTICAL ANALYSIS IN NONBELIEF: THE UNITED STATES AND INTERNATIONAL TRENDS

In March of 2015, the Barna Group published their State of Atheism in America report.[42] Barna is a religiously focused research organization that documents faith and nonfaith trends in the United
States. Their research found that the "non-Churched," those they
categorize as skeptics and who fit the atheist or agnostic profile
make up 25 percent of people who choose not to attend house of

worship services. The other 75 percent are people who may be spiritual but who have not declared a faith. The second statistic denotes that this group avoids house of worship services for three main reasons: like the skeptics, (1) they share a lack of trust in Church leadership, (2) they believe that church teachings are unfair or outright cruel to minority groups like the LGBT community, or (3) they accept the idea that morality, ethics and empathy come from within rather than through external sources such as a holy book.

Barna also found that the skeptic profile continues to expand and includes many demographic groups. According to their research, 34 percent of Nones are under thirty years old. This is a 16 percent increase since 1993. In 2015, they found that Nones are now largely college-educated—an increase from 33 percent to 50 percent—and that 43 percent of Nones are women, which is a 16 percent increase from 1993. Barna's research also suggests that as a group, Nones are more racially diverse and are more dispersed across the nation than in previous surveys. This data indicates that nonbelief is not only rising in the United States but that skepticism is no longer quartered in the big cities or among certain demographic groups. Skeptics and nonbelievers, regardless of what they're called, are everywhere.

Trinity College's study of American nonbelievers shows that 60 percent of those who claim no faith are male, while 40 percent are female.[43] In addition, 72 percent of nonbelievers are between the ages of 18-69 years old and 45 percent of "Nones" are married compared to 53 percent of the general population. Single, never married, divorced or widowed make up 53 percent of nonbelievers compared to 45 percent of believers in this category. Among those who do not believe, 72 percent are white, while blacks and Hispanics make up 20 percent of the ethnicities listed in the study. Fifty-five percent of those nonbelievers surveyed have attended some college or have attained degrees through post-graduate studies and 43 percent have high school or less than high school equivalency.

According to that same study, income distribution amongst those with faith as compared to those without belief is close to equal which suggests that on average income is not necessary a primary qualifier for either belief or nonbelief. Strikingly, 32 percent of those surveyed who identified as nonbelievers knew they were atheists by the age of twelve. Evolution was accepted by 65 percent of American "Nones" compared to the 38 percent of religious believers who accept evolution.

The 2012 Win-Gallup survey on global religion and nonbelief demographics showed that of the total who consider themselves believers, atheists or nonbelievers, 36 percent are male and 37 percent are female (the remaining percentage did not respond to the gender question). Further, 70 percent are age fifty or younger. In terms of education, 43 percent of the faithless in this survey had gone to college. Monthly household income levels between the faithful and those without faith also seem to be in parity. There appears to be a close-to-even split in all income categories.[44]

For example, in the highest economic quintile, 49 percent of those surveyed were religious while those who were not religious or without any faith made up 46 percent. However, the research found the fewest atheists to be in the lowest economic quintile. So, of the poorest group, 66 percent were confirmed believers while 28 percent were nonbelievers.

The year 2013 saw new research on possible atheist personality traits in a paper published by sociologist Christopher F. Silver of the University of Tennessee.[45] His research suggests that there is a spectrum of six fundamental personality groupings of those who claim to be nonbelievers. His categories and our definitions are:

- **Intellectual/Agnostics**—those who enjoy discussing their atheism as an academic or philosophical subject.

- **Activist Atheists**—the category of people profiled in this book who define their need to be activists by their atheist viewpoint.

- **Seeker-Agnostics**—those who do not believe but also do not challenge the faithful.

- **Anti-Theists**—those who do not believe and do seek out and challenge the faithful.

- **Nontheists**—those who have no belief and do not think about believers much. Nonbelievers who aren't concerned with what nonbelievers think or believe.

- **Ritual Atheists**—those who do not believe but still participate in religious ritual on occasion and may even belong to a house of worship, especially if one's partner, family, or community continues to have ties to a faith community.

While these broad groupings can encapsulate nonbelievers, we may, depending on our situation or environment, be categorized by many of these labels at once, or perhaps none at all. While this is new research and more work needs to be done, this preliminary data may help shed light as to the broader personalities and motivations of atheists as a demographic group.

ATHEISM & HUMANISM: BELIEF VERSUS CONCLUSION

Atheism and humanism are currently defined, in whole or in part, by the non-acceptance of a personal or communal deity. Neither accepts, without firm and reproducible evidence, a supernatural explanation or cause for the creation of life, the universe or any aspect of existence. From our research it appears atheists and humanists come to nonbelief in two distinct ways, but we acknowledge that there may be other roads traveled which allows one to arrive at nonbelief. Based on our interviews we find that these nonbelievers have either never had faith although they may or may not have been reared and nurtured in a home where faith and religious ritual was accepted, or they had faith because they grew up in a home where it was accepted but broke with it through their own process experience and discovery.

As seen from our interviews, belief resulting from authority can be a powerful force in bringing someone to believe in God or serve within a faith community, but such emotional force is not empirical evidence for God. Philosopher Mathew McCormick said, "The religious goal of fostering belief is at odds with the epistemological goal of believing only those conclusions that are justified by the evidence."[46] So, we find that atheists and humanists are driven by the need for rational proof and evidence to feed their skepticism. Without verifiable proof, those who are atheists conclude that not only is there no God, but that the God concept is in itself solely an ancient human contrivance which evolved as humans evolved both morphologically and culturally.

In contrast, religious belief is the opposite of evidence-based thinking. Belief requires no rational scheme to produce ideas. Holding a religious belief or a variety of supernatural ideas is an emotional and psychosocial response to one's culture, community, experience, and/or indoctrination. This belief response can be based on commitment, love, fear of eternal damnation, or any other of a host of emotions and loyalties. But none of these beliefs or loyalties are based on factual evidence for God, which is what the atheists in this book all claim to need to justify acceptance of an almighty being. To most atheists, religions are hopes wrapped in wishes which are then fortified by religious doctrine and community. In the end, an argument is valid when the truth of the premises entails the truth of the conclusions.

CONCLUSIONS

The atheists we've met in this book are essentially the same people who you see every day walking their dog, eating in restaurants, shopping in stores. But the one thing that sets these interviewees apart, even from their nonbelieving peers, is the desire to change the world in some way by helping others.

Atheism is growing. This growth is moving people from all cultural and demographic groups to a more secular world view. In the last decade alone, the group of people under thirty has seen the largest and most sustained growth in nonfaith adherents, but nonbelief amongst the older sectors of the population is also on the rise.

The northern European nations of Denmark, Sweden, Holland and Norway have the most citizens who live without the need for a personal deity. However, many other nations, larger and less homogeneous, including nations in Central and South America, Europe, Asia, the Middle East and Africa are also moving to this conclusion. In the United States, the number of faithless has grown to more than sixty-five million people and is still rising.

Those who have no belief in a personal God can, and do, work in all fields, trades, and disciplines. There appears not to be any bias in terms of the careers atheists enter to make a living. Even those who are former pastors and who have given up their flocks and the altar have come out of the closet to express, and in some cases shout vigorously their nonbelief in the supernatural. Nonbelief is the third largest and fastest growing "belief system" on the planet today.

......

"I'm actually an atheist."
REBECCA VITSMUN
when asked by CNN's Wolf Blitzer
if she thanked the Lord for
saving her family after
a devastating tornado leveled their
Oklahoma home in 2013

CHAPTER 7

....

WHERE NONBELIEVERS STAND AND WHERE THE MOVEMENT MAY GO NEXT

THE ADVENT OF ONLINE ACTIVISM

The world is filled with more than a billion people who do not believe in a god. As seen in this book and from what we know from speaking to our friends and other colleagues in the non-belief movement, both political secularism and activism are happening all around us. Although these facts may seem surprising, the reality is that faith-based ways of living have been challenged since the dawn of our human history. Doubt and skepticism are each healthy, and they are the core reasons why many atheists live evidenced-based lives.

Critics of faith have written their doubts on everything from vellum, to parchment, to paper and now electronically on websites and blogs. The wonderful thing about our current use of computers and networks is that they allow both writer and reader almost instant access to shared ideas despite time and distance. Can you imagine if Robert Ingersoll, the nineteenth century critic of faith, had the Internet to share his ideas? This man was perhaps the Christopher Hitchens of his day and lived a century before social media. Ingersoll's exploits were captured in newspapers across the United States and Europe as he would debate in favor of secularism and atheism and consistently win against the clergy and accomodationist intelligentsia opponents that he faced.[47]

The founder of American Atheists, Madalyn Murray O'Hair, was a dramatic and frank secular activist who was proclaimed in a 1964 issue of *LIFE* Magazine to be "The Most Hated Woman in America" because of her outspoken advocacy for secularism and the civil rights of nonbelievers.[48] She too was known for not taking prisoners when challenging the faithful to prove their views. While her written works are still available and her television interviews can be found online, she was a woman before her time, using the airwaves to vocally demand fairness for nonbelievers, even if in the process she was vilified and chastised for her outspokenness and ideas.

The Internet and social networking sites like Facebook, Twitter, and Meetup.com have each helped join complete strangers to secularism and nonbelief and thus have served as both social and political catalyst for activism. The digital world has cemented our movement and given leaders access to share ideas which have allowed atheist, skeptic, and secular humanist groups to sprout up around the world. Whether large or small, each group typically works to raise awareness about the positive nature of nonbelief and humanistic secularism. In the process, each activist and group collectively ensures that secular and atheist voices can be heard everywhere, from main street to city hall to the halls of Congress. But equally and perhaps even more importantly nonbelief groups can also serve to reach out to those feeling isolated, and those who want to listen and join in the struggle for secular civil rights.

THE LEGAL STRUGGLE FOR SCIENCE, REASON AND SECULARISM

At the quarter point of the twentieth century in America, we saw a turn from the philosophical debate about nonbelief and evolution become a legal one about science education and secularism. The main challenges centered on Darwin's theories concerning evolution, humanity's place in nature, and the constitutional separation of church and state.

In the United States, where religion and faith remain central to our politics, the challenge to teaching evolution continues to rear its ugly head in communities around the nation. Fortunately, our laws are based on precedent. We take the final outcome of the now famous Scopes Monkey Trial, where Tennessee high school science teacher John Scopes was found guilty, fined and later acquitted of violating the Butler Act, a statute which forbade the teaching of biological evolution, as an affirmation, if only inadvertent, of the separation of church and state.[49] Since Scopes, other legal decisions handed down by judges continue to side with the constitution. In the famous 2005 *Kitzmiller v. Dover Area School District* case in Pennsylvania, Judge John E. Jones III, found that teaching anything but scientific facts, such as creationism and "intelligent design," violates the constitution's establishment clause.[50]

Other legal challenges regarding the assumed right of the faithful to encroach on secular society have ensued, including public disputes about Ten Commandments monuments in public courts and the symbolism of Judeo-Christian iconography in public schools, on public roads, and in public open space.

Most recently the 911 Miracle Cross battle continues in our courts. The trustees and caretakers of the 9/11 museum plan to display a thirty-foot steel T-beam from the fallen World Trade Center that looks like a cross. This object was sanctified by priests and has become a religious icon. Those suing to keep the cross out believe that to exhibit it in the museum, which is partially funded by tax dollars, will add an unnecessary religious dimension to the terrible events of September 11, 2001. The plaintiffs also argue that such a display violates the separation clause of the Constitution and makes it almost impossible for many nonbelievers to go to the museum without feeling marginalized. In July of 2014, the Second Circuit Court threw the case out, stating the "Cross was about history and hope and not about religion."[51]

If we consider that the terrorist attacks were indeed a drastic but not unexpected form of religious terrorism and violence, it is sadly ironic to see a religious symbol placed within this publicly funded space. After all, people from many non-Christian religions also died in the attacks. Do we not sully their memory when we place such specific religious iconography in a public museum that is reserved for every American?

Activism Is The Key

As the legal wins and losses mount and lessons are learned from these activities, a large portion of our focus for the future concerning secular civil rights should be on the next generation of activists, on those nonbelievers who pursue their constitutional rights and who also perform acts of public service.

For the atheist and secular humanist movement to remain vibrant we have to harness the energies and optimism of those now in school. This is a key demographic and data suggests that as the "Nones" grow in number so too will their need to feel connected to others who are likeminded.

We should laud the efforts of students like Jessica Ahlquist of Rhode Island who sued to have a written religious prayer removed from her high school's auditorium.[52] And we have to support Matthew LaClair from Kearny, New Jersey, who audiotaped his high school social studies teacher stating that those did not accept Jesus were going to hell, that dinosaurs and humans lived at the same time, and that there was no proof of evolution.[53] We also have to stand with sophomore Gage Pulliam from Oklahoma, who in 2013 sued to have the Ten Commandments removed from each classroom in his pubic high school.[54]

Many of these students have brought civil suits. They have done so with their parents support and had legal defense sponsored by atheist organizations, private legal firms, and in some cases the ACLU or the American Humanist Association.

In colleges and high schools around the United States, the Secular Student Alliance, and related nonbeliever student groups are doing advocacy and community work to help others and at the same time they're activating the next generation of atheists, agnostics and skeptics. Around the world similar secular youth groups are attempting to transform autocratic republics in Asia and the Middle East and reframe secularism in the formerly communist nations of Eastern Europe. There are students who by their own efforts and hard work are going into nations where churches have had a monopoly on how charity is defined and are providing the same services without the need for recipients to pray or accept a Bible as part of the process of receiving food, shelter, medical or other community-building support.

SOME PITFALLS OF FAITH-BASED
HUMANITARIANISM

Most of the activists interviewed for our book have a very dim view of faith and see it as antithetical to human happiness and justice. Many of the profiled humanitarians have come to experience theology not as a positive force for good, or have had experiences leading them to the conclusion that organized faith is perhaps even dangerous and counterintuitive to human happiness. For the former clergy who are now humanist and atheist activists, it was a universal sentiment that the caustic nature of faith had actually worsened the suffering of others. For instance, they mention the Catholic Church's efforts in blocking the distribution of condoms which have been proven to prevent the spread of STDs and AIDS and to help manage birthrates. There's harm done by certain evangelical or other religious groups who enforce and support dogmatic and sometimes violent anti-women or anti-LGBT laws, or by whole communities or nations which actively attempt to block or ban secularist rights and the teaching of evolution.

In some cases, these organized faiths and their supporters are part of a cycle of corruption, have served as informers, or have themselves used their political connections to bully others. And in some cases, they've actually supported state violence in order to keep secularists fearful and afraid for their own lives, or their family and community's wellbeing.

Others profiled acknowledge that they have friends and colleagues who are religious and who also may be working for religious organizations that are trying to save lives, build communities, and support the self-sufficiency of others devastated by either manmade or natural disasters. Many of these interviewees, those who consider themselves "bridge-builders" between secular and faith communities, lauded the efforts of their religious comrades. And they, like the authors, see the value of sincerely helping in the name of humanity regardless of one's personal beliefs or ideals.

But some view doing humanitarian work in the name of God as being both disingenuous and counterproductive. In their view, it is nearly impossible to act humanistically in the name of faith even if those taking such action are true believers, simply because most faiths bring with them a ministry or missionary component—an impossible leap for those who choose not to believe in any deity or faith doctrine. They also see a real moral evil in forcing people without any means, perhaps in poor health and many times living in devastated communities, to accept Bibles, conduct prayer services, or participate in religious ritual. Some observed that when religious organizations do help people they frequently attempt to link their specific faith to their efforts or support it through branding, the wearing of religious T-shirts, the hanging of banners, and the handing out of leaflets, religious objects or trinkets. This becomes a cultural way of life as the people needing help and the religion needing adherents enter a partnership for their own mutual benefit. However, those activists who have seen this first-hand see it as less of an equal partnership and more one of dominance by the faith organization. In its most extreme sense, as one of the former clergy points out, it's a form of religious imperialism and subjugation in the guise of love, faith, and charity.

For many of the interviewees, though their nonbelief informs their political views, their social views and their humanitarian actions, they conclude that when they help those in need, they do so without tacitly asking for those in need to first accept, even casually, their personal beliefs, values or ideas.

The Case For Collective Secular Action: The Reason Rally

The year 2012 was a banner year for both secularism and nonbelief. Major organizations, activists, speakers, funders, and lay individuals came together for what was the first largescale celebration of nonbelief and secular activism. The Reason Rally, held in March 2012 on the National Mall in Washington, DC, was a three-day event that brought together people from around the United States and also from the international freethought community, where they stood together for political and social secularism.[55]

The Reason Rally began as a movement-wide event sponsored by the country's major secular organizations. The goal and objectives were (and remain) to unify, energize, and embolden secular people across the United States. At the same time, participants sought to dispel the negative opinions held by many Americans, and the belief that nonbelievers are immoral and harmful to America's future growth, prosperity and security.

While many people remember those rainy days as a kind of Woodstock for freethinkers, some serious politicking occurred days before the Rally took place. Dozens of activists came early to meet with their legislators and to discuss secular issues that are important to our community. As a voting group, nonbelievers have suffered from a lack of organization. The Reason Rally was meant to change the conversation in Congress and stem the tide of real and perceived balkanization.

In previous election cycles, officials have been more afraid of upsetting religious and evangelical voters than the thirty-seven million nonbelievers (about 15 percent of the US population). As a combined group, secularists are larger than many of the more vocal religious groups that fund candidate election or re-election campaigns. But silence and lack of organization rarely brings positive political results. This is why we must speak to our legislators. Perhaps this is also why even the allies that nonbelievers have in Congress won't come out. However, this is changing—notably with the entry of the Freethought Equality fund, a PAC established to increase the number of openly humanist and atheist elected officials at all levels of public office. This is an especially important change because with the exclusion of former Congressman Peter Stark, no sitting member of Congress has revealed that they're either a freethinker, atheist, humanist or other class of nonbeliever; yet we know that there must be many who serve in Washington and beyond.

The Reason Rally has helped to energize a movement that was already growing. It served notice to legislators and those faithful who work to make this nation and the world more deeply religious that nonbelievers, no matter how they identify, will no longer be quiet. In fact, they are organizing more efficiently and effectively, raising funds, and taking political, legal and social action every day. The days where secular organizations had to go hat-in-hand to political representatives and ask to be heard appear to be over. These groups are now demanding to be listened to by our fellow Americans and those elected officials who have the power to write and approve legislation that could potentially impact all nonbelievers and secularists alike.

The Right Not To Believe
As The Next Great
Civil Rights Movement

Secular driven politics is remaking society in the United States and throughout Europe through social movements and laws that guarantee human and civil rights to all citizens. These rights include access to medical care, universal education, economic and elder-care support, and labor laws which ensure fair wages and a level playing field in hiring. There is press freedom, a growing right to love and marry whom one wishes, and the right to have religious faith as well as to express no religious or spiritual belief.

Until the mid-twentieth century in the United States, atheists, humanists and other nonbelievers mostly remained in the closet, too afraid to be honest with themselves, their families, and their communities. Some activists in the movement, such as atheist blogger Greta Christina, speculate that the atheist movement needs its own Stonewall or Triangle Shirtwaist Fire or Freedom Summer to fully come into its own. However, we, and many others accept that the political, social and organizational steps taken to date by secular activists make such events unnecessary to duplicate. Especially since the loss of any life to violence, inaction, or ignorance only harms our communities and our social commitment to each other.

However, many of those who remain in the atheist closet have good reason to be fearful. In the United States, more people are likely to cast a presidential vote for a convicted felon or for a variety of other "outgroups" (Muslims, Mormons, Jews) than an atheist.[56] The most popular reason given for this dislike usually comes in the form of "Atheists don't share my values."[57] To our fault, we've let others define nonbelievers and nonbelief. These unfair and negative stereotypes, long since imparted and constantly used to ensure our illegitimacy, have stuck in the minds of the masses. We have to confront these perceptions and win the war of ideas and ideals.

But in real terms, this means nonbelievers have been discriminated against. We've heard many stories of people losing their jobs because of their atheism. Or nonbelievers have lost the respect of family members or their entire social network or communities. In fact, in thirteen nations on the planet if you admit to being an atheist, you can be put to death for blasphemy. In the United States, while the death penalty is off the table, the faithless still suffer in social isolation. As noted by former first lady and past secretary of state, Hilary Clinton, "It is time to overcome the false divide that pits religious sensitivities against freedom of expression and pursue a new approach based on concrete steps to fight intolerance wherever it occurs."[58]

If you should happen to live in the Northeast or the West Coast, you can be more open and comfortable with your atheism. However, if you live in either the South or Midwest, keeping your identity as a nonbeliever closed almost seems advisable as a form of self-preservation and personal security.

But the goal for many politically involved organizations in the US, like American Atheists, the Freedom from Religion Foundation, the American Humanist Association, and the Secular Coalition for America, is to help individuals as well as affiliated and allied organizations turn the tide of American ignorance and hostility towards nonbelievers into one of respect and inclusion. Through numerous educational campaigns, these organizations have covered the nation in billboards that say it's OK to be a nonbeliever. These activities have been duplicated internationally by other nations' nonbelief groups and organizations. In doing so each hopes to bring those still fearful an opportunity to stand in the light and to be counted. In addition, these agencies have advertised on television, radio, and the Internet, supported political action committees, taken to the skies with banners and gone to the airwaves to meet ignorance with facts, all the while continuing to meet with conservative and liberal legislators.

It is through the political will to understand, adapt, speak out and work to serve others that we bring the civil rights of atheists and the human rights of all people together as one human family—allowing all our children to grow and become full adults in a world without fear of oppression—where each of us can be and will be good without any god.

·····•···

The time to be happy is now.
The place to be happy is here.
The way to be happy is to make others so.

–POLITICIAN/ORATOR ROBERT GREEN INGERSALL

CHAPTER 8

CONCLUSIONS

ON IDENTITY AND ACTIVISM

L oneliness is unbearable for most people. Humans are social animals. And humans are not comfortable with ontological uncertainty. We cast around for answers and meaning, and whether we think we find those answers in a god or in science, we still have to live with the incompleteness of not knowing. We have to live with the limits of our consciousness, and with the challenge of death. Terror management is not for the faint of heart. And to navigate that terror with grace is nothing short of an art form.

Atheism is a brave choice. Not only because it often results in ostracism and derision for the atheist, but also because, as atheists, we have to swim in those scary waters without a clear coast in sight.

We hope by introducing you to some atheists who not only manage this great unknown, but also find great meaning in helping their fellow travelers, that we've helped to lessen the unnecessary divide between those who manage their lives through religious affiliation and those who don't.

We conclude that those profiled exhibit strong internalized beliefs regarding their self-image as it relates to humanitarian and secular action. These internalized ideas form the core of their activism. In most cases, they see themselves as servants to and for humanity—people who do their good work not to please any gods, but to benefit all humans and other beings on the planet. As a multi-ethnic and multi-regional global group, they have all externalized their humanitarianism and used the secular humanist code to inform their morality and ethics.

The profiled secular humanitarians have firmly defined this secular code in their private lives. And two personal yet foundational conclusions can be drawn from their work. The first conclusion is that there is no evidence for God. Some of the interviewees who accept the idea of a universe devoid of any deity never had religious faith to begin with. Others were born into families where the practice of religion was deeply important, and at some point their skepticism ultimately rejected faith as being unnecessary or outmoded.

The second conclusion is the idea that in order to make the world a better, kinder and safer place, individual and collective action is required. For many, this secular calling was and is the highest moral value they could place on their lives.

GODLESS GRACE

Those who offered their time, attention, perspectives and personal stories for our book were willing to do so because they know what we know: the more people read about atheists, secular humanists and other nonbelieving activists, the more the negative stereotypes about nonbelief and nonbelievers will diminish. Their actions show that grace can and does come from the godless and that theological guidance is not essential for empathy, altruism, meaning, or love. For those who believe it is, we hope you will become less fearful of us nonbelievers and realize that there are good and bad among us all, whatever our beliefs. The ontological war is not between the religious and the nonreligious but between good and evil, and the answers lie in ethical deeds, not just in beliefs. Or as Bertrand Russell noted, "love of god is replaced by worship of the ideal good."[59]

Afterword

BY DAVID SILVERMAN, PRESIDENT,
AMERICAN ATHEISTS, INC.

I remember my first experience as an atheist activist, in 1997, in Washington, DC. The Promise Keepers were in town and I traveled down from New Jersey to meet up with the American Atheists—a group of which I'd heard a few times before. The planned picket of the Promise Keepers march was preceded the evening before by a press conference attended by very little press, yet it was an important event in my life. It was the first time I walked into a room full of atheists. I made friends with brilliant and passionate people that night and my life was changed forever.

Shortly thereafter I attended my first atheist convention, and I learned how hated nonbelievers were, even by the people we were paying for the meeting space. First, we needed to find a hotel that would allow a group of atheists to gather there (and pay retail), and when we did, the hotel would not place the words "American Atheists" on the directory of events in the hotel—they listed us only as "AA." In fact, if someone called the hotel asking if the atheists were gathering there, the hotel said "no." (It's hard to run an event like that.)

That was 1997. Now fast forward.

In 2013, Kansas City, that is the city of Kansas City, contacted me to solicit the American Atheists National Convention. They wanted us bad. They offered me a round-trip airfare, tickets to a Bon Jovi concert, and VIP seats at a Royals game. When I told them I couldn't accept because it was my daughter's birthday, they told me to bring her, so I did, and we were both given a great treatment by a Bible-Belt city that wanted that atheist business. Food, booze, the works.

Why? What changed?

Business, like politics and entertainment, is reflexive, not active. Business (unlike businesspeople) has no bigotry—it seeks money. In 1997, nobody thought atheism had any money, because nobody thought atheists existed. Now, after the explosive growth of the movement, the Reason Rally, and the incredible increase in exposure we've received over the past few years, all that has changed, and we are being recognized as the influential and sizeable movement we are. For anyone wondering about the efficacy of our movement, you need only look at the change in the number of people who solicit our business over the past few years—to say nothing of how it was in the days of Madalyn Murray O'Hair.

And it all goes up from here. Nationwide, poll after poll shows that not only is atheism rising, it is rising faster than all religions, in all fifty states. Moreover, atheism as it is correlated to youth in most polls, shows that the younger you are, the more likely it is that you're an atheist. This means that as the population ages, the more religious old people will die out, leaving the less religious young folk behind. And this means that the growth of atheism is being helped by both the increase of information, and time itself. That's two very powerful forces helping the growth of atheism in the coming several years, which will yield the continued and increasing growth of atheism in America.

All we need to do is manage it, so we can take advantage of our size and combined dedication to establish a permanent and thriving place for atheists at America's table. We are well on our way, and we will succeed in our lifetime. That is, if we are able to take advantage of our imminent and continuing growth through the final throes of religion's dying privilege.

That's where you come in. You, dear reader, are vital to our success. Our growth is great, and inevitable, but that does not mean we will win our fight for equality nationwide. We need to flex our political and social muscles. We need to raise our voice. We need to show that we care enough to use the power and size that is coming.

We could still lose, and make no mistake; we definitely will lose, if atheists stay in the closet, if atheists stay quiet, if we worry more about upsetting the theists than we care about our own equality.

Silence kills movements. It implies not only acquiescence, but also endorsement. If you stay quiet, you stay marginalized, and you tell people you like it.

Well, do you?

CRITICAL THINKING & DISCUSSION QUESTIONS

This book is intended to raise the discussion of what it means to do humanitarian work without religious faith as the basis for doing good. We realize that a work of this type can serve a general as well as an academic or theological purpose to foster discussion at home, in a book club, house of worship or in a classroom setting. These critical-thinking questions are meant to enhance and focus such discussion but they are certainly not the only questions which one could ask when thinking about being "good without a god."

SUGGESTED QUESTIONS
CHAPTERS 1, 2 AND 3
INTERVIEWS WITH NONBELIEVING HUMANITARIAN ACTIVISTS

- How do the atheists interviewed relate to and view religious faith? How are the views similar and how do they differ?
- Do you agree or disagree with how they view faith? Does one view resonate with you? Why?
- Why do you think the atheists in this section view religion the way they do?
- Can you take the arguments that the interviewees make about faith and apply them to nonbelief?
- Would you consider faith without religious dogma a possible answer to the concerns of the atheists in this chapter?
- Can you suggest additional reasons why atheists may feel so strongly about their beliefs?
- There is a philosophical argument which states that atheism is just another form of religion. Do you agree or disagree with this idea?
- Do you have beliefs which are not religious or atheistic but which drive you to specific purposes or to help others?
- Do you think a nontheistic perspective is valuable for helping solve the world's problems and issues?

- Has your life or those in your family or community been affected by someone in the nontheist community? Was it a positive or negative experience?
- Does atheism make the holder of such beliefs a stronger or weaker individual?
- Why do you think the people interviewed felt their atheism made them want to make a difference and enter public service?
- How differently did you think the conclusions made by those in this chapter differ from religious activists?
- A primary call to action for many of the nonbeleivers in these chapters focuses on the conclusion that we only live once. Does this view offer enough insight into their motivations?
- If atheism weren't an option, which way of being or philosophy do you think would be the most appealing to the atheists in this chapter?

CHAPTER 4
BACKGROUND & HISTORY ON WORD MEANINGS, ATHEISM AND HUMANISM

- What can we learn from those philosophers and historians who were themselves freethinkers and atheists?
- Can we make the case that the concept of atheism is an ancient form of knowing and experiencing the world?
- Do you think nonbelief, as a form of philosophy, can truly motivate people to social action?
- Are there people in your life or community who are themselves nonbelievers, atheists, humanists, or skeptics?
- How did Hume, Spinoza, and Darwin view religion in their own time and how do those ideas impact our current view?

CHAPTER 5
WHO ARE THE ATHEISTS

- Based on the evidence presented in this book, would you conclude that modern atheism is a worldwide phenomenon?
- Why do you think there is such a diversity of people in the freethought movement today?
- Why are we able to define the concept of atheism easily, but perhaps not recognize atheists and their values?
- As a growing population of nonbelievers, how do you think the New Atheist Movement will grow and change within the next decade?

- Do you believe atheists can help or hurt causes because of their beliefs?

CHAPTER 6—WHERE ARE THE ATHEISTS?

- Do you accept or reject the ideas and opinions of the nonbelievers closest to you? Why?
- Should atheists remain "in the closet" rather than freely express their ideas?
- If you were an atheist, would you be inclined to share your ideas and beliefs?
- Activist atheists are on every continent and in almost every country. Do you think this helps or hinders the causes they support?
- Do you think that atheists and the faithful can work together successfully in times of human-caused or natural disasters?

CHAPTER 7
WHERE THE MOVEMENT MAY BE HEADED

- Do you agree or disagree with the statement "Secular rights may be the next great civil rights movement"?
- Can you think of alternative scenarios where the humanist and atheist movement may grow or recede?
- What political, social, or economic impacts could you expect in the future if the should secular civil rights movement became more actively legislated (for or against) as a Constitutional or equal rights issue?

CHAPTER 8—CONCLUSIONS

- Why do you think atheists take action based on their nonbelief and secular conclusions?
- Would you work for an NGO, nonprofit, or other relief agency if you knew it was managed by atheists?
- Do you think the number of secular and religious aid organizations is appropriate for the global needs for support?
- Could the atheists in this chapter have worked effectively if they belonged to faith-based aid organizations?
- Do nonbeliever aspirations and work have value? Could this work be done in the same way if it were done for other causes or reasons?

Resources For Humanists, Freethinkers And Humanitarian Activists

For all the activists we've had the pleasure of meeting, interviewing, and profiling, we know that there are still many more people who would like to participate in humanist and activist work. All participation has value even if you don't have a lot of time or other resources to give. Because so many organizations rely on volunteer hours to help provide services there aren't many who would turn away a helping hand.

Helping others also provides opportunities to meet likeminded people. As you provide humanitarian support to others or help the natural environment, it is almost impossible to imagine that you will not grow emotionally because of your humanist work.

With this personal growth will come opportunities to lead others and gain deeper satisfaction in making our world safer, richer and kinder. As an informal lay leader or as an elected member to a group, you'll also have the opportunity to mentor those who are just coming into their own, who recognize that healing the world and helping others is noble, and that doing such work in the name of humanity is probably the best option all humans can pursue.

Organizations listed here have been collected by scouring various print and online sources and directories. It is not complete and the information will eventually become old or otherwise outdated. We recommend that you use this section as a jumping-off point and look to national and international organizations which can help you find freethought groups in your area. We'd also recommend looking at social media sites and websites like Meetup.com, to find activist groups and organizations doing non-faith-based humanitarian work in your area.

This is an alphabetical list of international humanist, secular, atheist and freethought organizations, many of which advocate for and assist those in need, and support secular charities and their allied services. Individually or in partnership they may direct aid groups or support the work of activists or other organized aid groups. This list also includes secular groups that work on and support environmental issues and secular civil rights issues.

SECULAR HUMANITARIAN RELIEF ORGANIZATIONS & AGENCIES		
ORGANIZATION NAME	SERVICE FOCUS	WEBSITE
American Civil Liberties Union (ACLU)	Legal/ Justice	www.aclu.org
American Red Cross	Disaster Relief	www.redcross.org
Amnesty International	Civil & Human Rights	www.amnesty.org
Atheists Helping the Homeless	Shelter Services	www.atheistshelping thehomeless.com
Camp Quest	Education	www.campquest.org
Doctors Without Borders	Disaster Relief/ Healthcare	www.doctorswithout borders.org
DonorsChoose.org	Public Education	www.donors choose.org
Electronic Frontier Foundation	Legal/Justice	www.eff.org
Engender Health	Healthcare & Population Control	www.engender health.org
Foundation Beyond Belief	Civil & Human Rights	www.foundation beyondbelief.org
Hivos	Civil & Human Rights	www.hivos.nl
Human Rights Campaign	Civil & Human Rights	www.hrc.org
Human Rights Watch	Civil & Human Rights	www.hrw.org
Kiva.org	Microfinance	www.kiva.org

SECULAR HUMANITARIAN RELIEF ORGANIZATIONS & AGENCIES CONTINUED		
ORGANIZATION NAME	SERVICE FOCUS	WEBSITE
Lambda Legal	Civil & Human Rights	www.lambdalegal.org
Mercycorps	Civil & Human Rights	www.mercycorps.org
National Center for Science Education	Environment & Science Education	www.ncse.com
The Nature Conservancy	Environment & Species Protection	www.nature.org
Network for Good	Crowd Source Funding	www1.network forgood.org
Oxfam International	Poverty Relief	www.oxfam.org
PlanUSA	Poverty Relief	www.planusa.org
Planned Parenthood Federation	Healthcare & Population Control	www.plannedparent hood.org
Population Connection Control	Healthcare & Population	www.population connection.org
Project Peanut Butter	Hunger Alleviation	www.project peanutbutter.org
Restore the Pledge	Legal/ Justice	www.restorethe pledge.org
Scouting for All	Legal Justice	www.scoutingforall.org
The SEED Foundation	Public Education	www.seed foundation.com
The Seva Foundation	Healthcare	www.seva.org
Southern Poverty Law Center	Legal/ Justice	www.splcenter.org
Texas Freedom Network	Civil & Human Rights	www.tfn.org
Treatment Action Campaign	HIV/ AIDS	www.tac.org.za
United Nations Children's Fund (UNICEF)	Social/Health/ Education Services	www.unicef.org
Union of Concerned Scientists	Environment & Science Education	www.ucsusa.org

INTERNATIONAL SECULAR, FREETHOUGHT, HUMANIST & ATHEIST ORGANIZATIONS		
ORGANIZATION NAME	SERVICE FOCUS	WEBSITE
Afghans Atheists Organization	Legal/Justice	www.facebook.com/Afghans-Atheists
American Atheists	Legal/Justice	www.americanatheists.org
American Ethical Union	Community Building	www.aeu.org
American Humanist Association	Legal/Justice	www.americanhumanist.org
Americans United for Separation of Church and State	Legal/Justice	www.au.org
Atheist Alliance International	Community Building	www.atheistalliance.org
Atheist Association of Finland	Community Building	www.dlc.fi/~etkirja/Atheist.htm
Atheist Centre of India	Civil & Human Rights	www.atheistcentre.in
Atheist Foundation of Australia	Community Building	www.atheistfoundation.org.au
Atheist Union of Greece	Community Building	union.atheia.gr
Atheist Ireland	Community Building	www.atheist.ie
Ateisti Srbije (Serbia)	Community Building	www.ateisti.com
Atheistisch Verbond (Netherlands)	Community Building	www.atheistischverbond.nl
Atheists of Spain	Community Building	www.iatea.org
Belgium Humanists	Community Building	www.h-vv.be
Black Atheists of America	Community Building	www.blackatheistsofamerica.com
Brazilian Association of Atheists & Agnostics	Community Building	www.atea.org.br
Brights	Community Building	www.the-brights.net
British Humanist Association	Community Building	www.humanism.org.uk

INTERNATIONAL SECULAR, FREETHOUGHT, HUMANIST & ATHEIST ORGANIZATIONS		
ORGANIZATION NAME	SERVICE FOCUS	WEBSITE
Center for Civil Courage (Croatia)	Legal/ Justice	www.civilcourage.hr
Center for Inquiry	Community Building	www.centerfor inquiry.net
Civil Association of Atheist (Czech Rep.)	Community Building	www.osacr.cz
Clergy Project	Community Building	www.clergyproject.org
Committee for the Scientific Investigation of Claims of the Paranormal Skeptical	Education	www.csicop.org
Council for Secular Humanism	Education	www.secular humanism.org
Denmark Atheists	Community Building	www.ateist.dk
European Humanist Federation	Community Building	www.humanist federation.eu
Feeding America	Poverty Relief	www.feeding america.org
Free Society Institute (South Africa)	Community Building	www.fsi.org.za
Freedom from Religion Foundation	Legal/Justice	www.ffrf.org
Freethinkers Association of Switzerland	Community Building	www.frei-denken. ch/de/
Freethought Lebanon	Legal/ Justice	www.freethought lebanon.net/
Gambia Secular Assembly	Community Building	www.gambia secularassembly.com
Humanist Alliance Philippines, International (HAPI)	Community Building	www.hapihumanist.org
Hofesh (Israel)	Legal/Justice	www.hofesh.org.il
Humanist Association of Canada	Community Building	www.humanist canada.ca/

INTERNATIONAL SECULAR, FREETHOUGHT, HUMANIST & ATHEIST ORGANIZATIONS		
ORGANIZATION NAME	SERVICE FOCUS	WEBSITE
Humanist Association of Ireland	Community Building	www.humanism.ie
Humanist Society of New Zealand	Community Building	www.humanist.org.nz
Humanist Society of Scotland	Community Building	www.humanism.scot
Humanist Society of Singapore	Community Building	www.humanist.org.sg
Humanist Society of Uganda	Education	www.haleauganda.org
Humanists of Germany	Community Building	www.humanismus.de
Humanists of Iceland	Community Building	www.sidmennt.is/ yfirlit-sidmennt
Humanists of Luxembourg	Community Building	www.aha.lu
Hispanic American Freethinkers	Community Building	www.hafree.org
Indonesian Atheists	Community Building	www.indonesian atheists.wordpress.com
Institute for Humanist Studies	Education	www.humanist studies.org
Interfaith Alliance	Community Building	www.interfaith alliance.org
International Humanist & Ethical Union	Community Building	www.iheu.org
International League of Non-Religious & Atheists (Germany)	Community Building	www.ibka.org
Iranian Atheists	Legal/Justice	www.iranian atheists.org
Malta Humanist Association	Community Building	www.malta humanist.org
Military Association of Atheists & Freethinker	Legal/Justice	www.military atheists.org
National Secular Society	Community Building	www.secularism.org.uk

INTERNATIONAL SECULAR, FREETHOUGHT, HUMANIST & ATHEIST ORGANIZATIONS		
ORGANIZATION NAME	**SERVICE FOCUS**	**WEBSITE**
Netherland Humanists	Community Building	www.humanist ischverbond.nl/
Nigerian Humanist Movement	Community Building	www.nigerian humanists.com
Norwegian Humanist Society	Community Building	www.human.no
Pakistani Atheists and Agnostics	Legal/ Justice	www.facebook.com/ Pakistani.Atheists
PATAS (Philippines)	Community Building	www.patas.co
People for the American Way	Legal/ Justice	www.pfaw.org
Polish Humanist Association	Community Building	www.humanizm.net.pl
Prometheus Society of Slovakia	Community Building	www.slovakia. humanists.net
Rational Response Squad	Education	www.rational responders.com
Rationalist Society	Community Building	www.rationalist. com.au
Rationalist Union of France	Education	iheu.org
Richard Dawkins Foundation for Reason & Science	Community Building	richard dawkins.net
Romanian Secular Humanist Society	Community Building	www.asur.ro
Russian Humanist Society	Community Building	www.humanism.ru
Secular Coalition for America	Legal/ Justice	www.secular.org
Secular Humanism Portugal	Community Building	humanism osecular.org
Secular Student Alliance	Community Building	www.secular students.org
Secular Woman	Community Building	www.secular woman.org

INTERNATIONAL SECULAR, FREETHOUGHT, HUMANIST & ATHEIST ORGANIZATIONS		
ORGANIZATION NAME	**SERVICE FOCUS**	**WEBSITE**
Skeptic Society	Education	www.skeptic.com
Society of Modern Atheism & Humanism (Russia)	Community Building	www.ateizm.su
Swedish Humanist Association	Community Building	www.humanisterna.se
Trinidad-Tobago Humanist Association	Community Building	www.humanist.org.tt
Union of Rationalist Atheists & Agnostics (Italy)	Community Building	www.uaar.it

Interview Questionnaire

Subject Interview Sheet

COUNTRY:

NAME

AGE   GENDER

OCCUPATION

QUESTIONS

- Were you ever religious? What is your background?
- Is/was there anyone in the non-faith community who shaped your world view?
- How has atheism shaped your work?
- How has atheism empowered you to see and change the world?
- Why doesn't faith or theism work for you?
- Why does atheism matter to you?
- Do you think your work could be done in the name of a deity?
- How is your work defined by your non-faith?
- What have you accomplished/want to accomplish?
- Would you recommend any books, websites, organizations for those who are interested in learning from you—as opposed to any religious resources?
- What questions have we not discussed and what do you want to share about yourself or your work that isn't covered by these questions?

SUPPLEMENTAL QUESTIONS

- What were/are your grandparents', parents' and siblings' beliefs?
- What are some of your morals and values as a nonbeliever?
- Is your society religious or not? Why?
- Were you taught about Darwin in school?
- Do you believe that people are essentially good?
- Do you have friends that are religious?
- If you have children, how would you feel if your kids became religious? Have they asked about God or what happens when we die?
- How do you think about and cope with death? Are you afraid to die, do you worry about it, what do you think happens after we die?
- What do you think is the meaning of life?
- How do you cope when things go wrong in your life? What do you do?
- What qualities are most important for you to foster in your children and family?

ENDNOTES

FORWARD

1   Jones, Jeffrey. 2012

2   Edgell, Penny 2006.

3   Id

4   Hwang, Karen 2011.

5   Furnham, Adrian, 1998

6   Volokh, Eugene. 2006

7   Harper, Marcel. 2007

INTRODUCTION

8   Simpson, J. and Weiner, C. [Eds.] (1989). *The Oxford English Dictionary*. Oxford: Clarendon Press.

9   Hitchens, Christopher (2007). *God is Not Great. How Religion Poisons Everything*. New York: Hatchett Book Group.

CHAPTER ONE

10 United Nations. (2006). Department of Public Information - News and Media Division. Rep. New York: United Nations

11 Tripathi, Salil. (2014). "Blogging, Blasphemy and Ban." Index of Censorship. Vol.24 N.1, pp119-122.

12 "Global Index of Religiosity and Atheism 2012." Win-Gallup International. Win-Gallup. 2012. Web. 2015.

13 Miller, Jon, Eugenie Scott and Shinji Okamoto. "Public Acceptance of Evolution." Science 313.5788 (2006): 765-766. Sciencemag.org. Science. www.sciencemag,org/content/313/5788/765.full.

CHAPTER THREE

14 www.law.unlv.edu/current-students/student-organization/sls.html

15 Gryboski, Michael (2012). "Atheist Students go to Church for Charitable Cause." *The Christian Post*. www.christianpost.com/news/atheist-students-go-to-church-for-charitable-cause-71862/

16 Martinez, Jessica (2013). "Christian Charity Rejects Atheists' Offer to Deliver Thanksgiving Meals; Group Deemed 'Unfit' to Help Share Gospel Message." *The Christian Post*. www.christianpost.com/news/christian-charity-rejects-atheists-offer-to-deliver-thanks-giving-meals-group-deemed-unfit-to-help-share-gospel-message-108808/

17 "Atheist Volunteers Snubbed by Soup Kitchen Will Restore Your Faith in Everything That's Good." (2013). *The Huffington Post*. www.huffingtonpost.com/2013/10/30/atheists-banned-soup-kitchen_n_4178443.html

18 Cheyne, James Allen. "Rise of the Nones and the Growth of Religious Indifference." (2010). *Skeptic Magazine*. Vol. 15, N. 4. http://www.arts.uwaterloo.ca/~acheyne/RAVS essays/essays/pdfs/Nones.pdf

CHAPTER FOUR

19 Long, A.A.[Ed.] (1999). The Cambridge Companion to Early Greek Philosophy. Cambridge: *Cambridge University Press.*

20 Roberson, J. (1936)]. *A History of Freethought, Ancient and Modern, to the Period of the French Revolution.* 4th ed.

21 O'Connor, Eugene (1993). *The Essential Epicurus letters, Principle Doctrines, Vatican Sayings and Fragments.* New York: Prometheus Books.

22 Fuhrman, Manfred (1992). Cicero and the Roman Republic. Massachusetts: Blackwell

23 Israel, Jonathan I. and Salversa, R. (2002). *Dutch Jewery: Its History and Secular Culture* (1500-2000). Leiden: Brill.

24 Interview with Albert Einstein, New York Times, 24 April 1921. Published 4/25/21.

25 Russell, R. (1995). *Freedom and Moral Sentiment: Hume's Way of Naturalizing Responsibility.* New York: Oxford University Press.

26 Pew Research Center (2012). "Nones" on the Rise. Religion & Public Life. 2012. www.pewforum.org/2012/10/09/nones-on-the-rise/

27 ID

CHAPTER FIVE

28 Grayling, A.C. (2013). The God Argument: The Case against Religion and for Humanism. New York: Bloomsbury

29 Knippenberg, Hans (2005). *The Changing Religious Landscape of Europe.* Amsterdam: Het Spinhuis.

30 Woodside, Cindy. "Statistically Speaking: Vatican Numbers Hint at Fading Faith Practice." *Catholic Reporter* [Kansas City]. 17 August 2012. 1.

31 Wilson, E.O. (1998). *Consilience: the Unity of Knowledge.* New York: Vintage Books.

32 Cooperman, Alan [Ed.] (2014). Global Religious Diversity: Half of the Most Religiously Diverse Countries Are in the Asia-Pacific Region. Rep. Comp. Conrad Hackett. Washington: Pew Research Center.

33 Galani, Ijaz [Ed.](2012). Win/Gallup Global Index of Religiosity and Atheism. Re. Comp. Rushna Shahid. London: Win/Gallup International.

34 Kishkovsky, Sophia, (2014). Putin in Ukraine to Celebrate a Christian Anniversary. The *New York Times.* Section A. Pg.4 (Citation 39). Oppenheimer, Mark (2014). Examining the growth of the 'Spiritual but not Religious." The *New York Times.* July 18, 2014. p.A14 (Citation 40).

35 Win/Gallup, supra n. 38

36 Downey, Allen B. Religious Affiliation, Education and Internet Use., *Cornell University.* Online. www.arvix.org/pdf/1403.553v1.pdf. 2014.

37 www.atheistnexus.org

INDEX

CPSIA information can be obtained
at www.ICGtesting.com
Printed in the USA
LVOW13s1522290318
571635LV00012B/676/P

9 780931 779633